MW01697548

1. Angels

THE ANGELS

MARIA PIA GIUDICI

The Angels

Spiritual and Exegetical Notes

Translated from the Italian
by
EDMUND C. LANE, SSP

ALBA · HOUSE alba house NEW · YORK
SOCIETY OF ST. PAUL, 2187 VICTORY BLVD., STATEN ISLAND, NEW YORK 10314

Italian edition published by Città Nuova Editrice under the title
Gli Angeli: Note esegetiche e spirituali.

Library of Congress Cataloging-in-Publication Data

Guidici, Maria Pia.
The angels: spiritual and exegetical notes / by Maria Pia Guidici. Translated from the Italian by Edmund C. Lane, SSP.
p. cm.
Includes bibliographical references.
ISBN 0-8189-0636-7 (alk. paper)
1. Angels. 2. Catholic Church — Doctrines. 3. Spiritual life — Catholic Church.
I. Title
BT966.2.G5813 1993
235'.3 — dc20 93-30849
CIP

Produced and designed in the United States of America by the Fathers and Brothers of the Society of St. Paul, 2187 Victory Boulevard, Staten Island, New York 10314, as part of their communications apostolate.

ISBN: 0-8189-0636-7

Printing Information:

Current Printing - first digit	2	3	4	5	6	7	8	9	10

Year of Current Printing - first year shown

1995 1996 1997 1998

CONTENTS

PREFACE

It takes all the faith, simplicity, zeal, and cultural background of a woman like Sister Maria Pia Giudici to write a book today that would have something worthwhile to say about the angels.

Angels! What purpose do they serve? Indeed, do they exist at all? Traditional belief in the angels has undergone three strong attacks in this century. A more enlightened and precise exegesis of the Scriptures, for example, would allow us to interpret the biblical "angels" as synonyms for God himself or for man. Psychology and, following it, modern ethnology has no trouble explaining the apparitions of the angels as a phenomenon (verifiable in many religions) of mythologization, of symbolic projection, of the expression of an imaginative animist mentality. Finally, a wholly rational and scientific explanation of things and of human beings, and of the way they influence one another, would probably find the existence, or at least the intervention, of invisible beings unacceptable and unnecessary.

The wonderful thing about this work of Sister Maria Pia is that she is fully aware of such objections and understands, on the one hand, that for the truth which they contain, they oblige us to a purer discernment (we don't have to see a real angel in all the passages of the Bible where the word "angel" appears); and, on the other hand, none of the three objections is truly "decisive," except for those who, having closed their minds to any reality that cannot be known by reason and science, reject faith and with it belief in many other things besides angels. But the Word of God (and above all that of Jesus himself), the Fathers of the Church, the common belief of centuries, the Magisterium and perhaps especially the liturgical life of the Church, invite the believer to embrace with admiration and joy these mysterious fellow creatures of almighty God, intelligent, free, loving, spiritual persons (about whose exact nature it is useless to discuss in great detail) "associated" with the divine plan for our salvation in dependence on Christ the sole Mediator.

The second great thing about these pages is that they enable us to perceive the perfect coherence of the mystery of the angels within the whole of the Christian mystery itself. The book traces the stages of the mystery as it unfolds. It discretely inquires into its various elements. Above all it resolutely concentrates on the key mystery of Christ as Redeemer. Every possibility of "angelolatry" is excluded (against which both St. Paul and St. John long ago were obliged to react). Christ's coming did not abolish the angels; but all the roles which they performed under the Old Law have now been assumed by him, the perfect Man! Their mediation continues to exist, but it has been assumed and sublimated in the one total mediation of the incarnate Son, who died and rose again from the dead. They have found their place and their definitive identity in him: they are the messengers of "the Body of Christ and its Head."

Seen in this light, the angels bring to our faith a help which is not inconsiderable: they allow us to better perceive "the unfathomable riches of Christ" (Ep 3:8), to better "understand the breadth, the length, the height, and the depth" of the "mystery," or eternal plan, of the Father (Ep 3:18).

A third praiseworthy thing about these reflections of Sister Maria Pia is that they lead us by the hand in a gradual way along the path to this discovery. They expand our horizons, make us understand how much greater God is than the human heart, refine our spiritual sensibilities, free us from the restrictions of rationalism and bring us to the contemplation of those "things unseen" whose reality we proclaim every Sunday in the Creed.

In effect, the angels, with their beatific existence, show forth the creative munificence of the Father and the full extent of his plan whose dimensions reach far beyond the merely "human." Through the angels we acknowledge, along with that of our own world and its multitude of human beings, that mysterious and probably immense universe of the "celestial host" which are the spiritual equivalent of the galaxies of stars which we contemplate by night and which shine "with joy for their Maker" (Bar 3:35). In their relationship with Christ and his Church, they manifest the breadth of the redemption and the transcendence of the Risen One in his personal as well as in his mystical Body. Subject to the Man-God, the sole Mediator, they offer their praise to the Father through him and receive from the Father their blessedness; they join with us in forming the Body of Christ and the family of the Father, not as "brothers and sisters" nor as "sons and daughters" (because the Word "was made flesh" and "became man" not an angel), but as "confidants," "associates," and "ministering spirits" (cf. Heb 1:14). They even exalt the greatness of Mary, the maiden from Nazareth who became the "Mother of God" and for that reason "Queen of Angels".

However, in their place and role, how great is their ardent and seraphic fervor, how dazzling their perfection! How much they can serve us as inspirers and infinitely exacting guides. Sister Maria Pia has rightfully been pleased to show how a lively faith and a steadfast invocation of the angels impacts on our daily life. These mysterious companions help us to remain sensitive to the dual dimension of God himself and to the fundamental dual task which corresponds to that.

God is *infinite Transcendence*: the first role of the angels is to contemplate, adore and praise Christ the Lord and through him the Father whose face they "continually look upon" (Mt 18:10). This is the very substance of their activity, the eternal ratification of their choice and gift of self made to divine Love. The Church links them with its own praise, or better yet, is associated with them in their praise, which is judged to be purer, more intense and everlasting. In this way a unique liturgy to the same Father through the same eternal High Priest is celebrated "on earth as it is in heaven." The angels represent a continual invitation to us to become contemplatives and adorers "in spirit and in truth."

God is also *salvific Condescension*: another role of the angels is to be our benefactors, in the name of Christ and of the Father, alongside and complementing the visible aid which the Church offers us. They support us in that most important stance of our faith which is to be open to the gifts of God. They assist us in receiving and understanding God's message, his special plan for us ("angel" means "messenger"). They accompany and protect us on the road as witnesses to the continual and loving providence of the Father. Finally, they help to free us from evil and from the Evil One, giving us that courage which all the members of the Church militant so need in their journey towards their heavenly homeland.

These are some of the riches which Sister Maria Pia offers us, exhibiting a vivacity of style, the finesse of a consecrated woman, and the experience of a spiritual guide to many brothers and sisters.

Those who read this book will sense in themselves a growing admiration for the munificence of God and will travel with greater trust along his path. Jesus himself has assured us that every time a Christian is converted and becomes a better Christian "there is joy in heaven among the angels of God" (Lk 15:10). What a wonderful thing it is to know that not only the saints but also the angels in heaven know me and follow my progress with love!

Joseph Aubry, Rome

INTRODUCTION

In the prologue of Luigi Santucci's play *Cain's Angel*, an angel appears in a spotlight on the darkened stage wrapped in a white tunic.

He addresses the spectators in these words: "You who are baptized, lend me your ears. In the drama about to unfold, I am the angel. Who are the angels? Does any one out there remember?" (There is a pause while the angel looks around the auditorium.) "I heard your thoughts. No. Not all those things. And not *only* those things." (Then, pointing here and there in the darkened hall, he continues.) "You thought about your mother. And you about your dead child. And the rest of you about celestial music, or a picture of a figure in white at the head of your bed.

"But it's right that you don't know. Perhaps you couldn't bear our presence if you thought that we were really there, next to you in every instant, *in every instant!* (...) Whether you think of us or not, we are with you, O Baptized, in the uncompromising and definitive way willed by God: always, always. Never distracted, never on vacation."[1]

I think it is significant that a contemporary writer of unquestioned reputation should underscore the reality of the

---

[1] L. Santucci, *L'Angelo di Caino* ["Cain's Angel"], Città Armoniosa, Reggio Emilia, Italy, 1977, p. 7.

angels without any hesitation whatsoever. That question, all the more provocative coming as it does at the beginning of the play, is in a way addressed to us all. We can almost hear it spoken — and why not? — by our own angel to each one of us: "Who are the angels? Does anyone out there remember?"

This book was written to respond to this question in a manner which is neither simplistic nor, I hope, presumptuous or separated from "today" in which the story of our salvation unfolds. With no attempt to cite a lot of critics or scholars, the book is nonetheless adequately documented. It gets its thrust from the serious questions which come up in the course of everyday living.

Thomas Angel Eliot is a student of computer sciences in the United States who has made a deep study of the laws behind these electronic brains. He is tireless in his efforts to perfect the specifications of this ever advancing technology, placing it at the service of upcoming generations. A short while back, for a combination of what might be called coincidental factors but which, to the contrary, are "graces of Providence," I came to know that he had written to his sister in Italy, who was pursuing her doctorate at the Pontifical Biblical Institute, asking her for some information about angels.

"Since I'm interested in a field which seeks to facilitate communications between people," he wrote, "I'd like to know something about the angels and to learn more about their mysterious influence, as messengers of God, on human beings."

For those whose mind's eye is clear and whose heart is observant, this, too, is a "sign of the times." It means that the cutting edge of scientific and technological progress is about to take on that "mountain" of prideful self-sufficiency which has so restricted the horizons of contemporary men and women, depriving them of spiritual oxygen. Mystery extends beyond those things which are rationally experimental and which can be catalogued under scientific categories alone.

At the summit — around, and within the world of reality

which can be seen and touched — is the barely perceptible, invisible but mysteriously wonderful world of the Spirit. When Pavel Evdokimov, in some lines of his anthropology, writes: "Man is determined from below and is challenged from on high. From his circle of limited possibilities arises an unlimited vertical dimension,"[2] he is implying a discourse on the reality of angels. Perhaps, precisely while some theologians remain "anchored" in the preconceptions of scientism, others are setting off towards the dimensions of the Spirit in the broadest sense of that term.

These pages are addressed to those precursors of a time which will be, in reaction to our own, the most spiritual ever to have appeared in the world as some have hypothesized (even if less spiritualistic!). They are addressed to those who allow themselves to be led by the movement of the Spirit until they become "true children of God" (Rm 8:14).

Someone recently published in an illustrated periodical (that voice and channel of the consumeristic mass-media mentality of our day) a "Secular Ten Commandments"[3] in which we find, among other things: "Abandon all pride [?] in being made in the image and likeness of God and of being able to aspire to eternal life." Then, after several other sardonic and hopeless assertions typical of many agnostics, we come across this strange flash of light, truer than the irony with which it was said: "Only if angels existed would your life (your life as a skeptic and an agnostic) be devoid of meaning."

Still, even this unexpected affirmation reveals how the angels represent, for many people today, only a nostalgic illusion or the mythical embellishment of a world totally abandoned along with their youth. But whoever, with a healthy

---

[2] P. Evdokimov, *La donna e la salvezza del mondo* ["Women and the Salvation of the World"], Jaka Books, Milan, 1980, p. 267.

[3] L. Firpo, *"Se i laicisti avessero un decalogo"* ["If Secularists Had a Ten Commandments"], in *Panorama*, July, 1981.

spiritual realism, wants to follow the side of Catholic truth and live within the amplitude of its vast horizons, will listen to another teacher.

The Second Vatican Council tells us that the Church has always "venerated [the apostles and martyrs], together with the Blessed Virgin Mary and the holy angels with a special love" (Dogmatic Constitution on the Church, *Lumen Gentium*, #50), which signifies that the recent Council considered devotion to the angels something taken for granted.

Pope Paul VI in his *Credo of the People of God* proclaims the Church's faith in "one God, Father, Son, and Holy Spirit, creator of things visible (such as this world in which our brief life runs its course) and of things invisible (such as the pure spirits which are also called angels)..."[4] And Pope John Paul I, the pope who passed like a meteor in the skies of the Church and the contemporary world, in the days when he was patriarch of Venice, wrote: "The angels are the great unknowns in these times with their tendency towards cosmolatry. Some have insinuated the doubt as to whether or not angels were persons. Many don't speak of them at all. It would, instead, be a good thing to remember them more often, as ministers of Providence in the governance of the world and of men, seeking to live in intimate familiarity with them as did the saints from Augustine to Newman."[5]

---

4 AAS 60 (1968), 436.

5 N. Costello, *"Cosí parlò papa Luciani da vescovo e cardinale"* ["Pope Luciani's Words as Bishop and Cardinal"], in *Il Carroccio* (Vigodarzere-Padua), 1980, p. 59.

THE ANGELS

1

ANGELS IN MODERN DAY CULTURE

1. *Do the Angels Exist? Affirmative and Demythologized Responses*

A quick trip through history among the oldest civilizations and religions will make us aware of one fact: everywhere there are traces of a belief in beings intermediate between the divine and the human.

Among primitive peoples, to every manifestation of nature there corresponded a spirit which was either good or bad depending upon the effect produced by such a phenomenon.

Behind every mountain and stream, certain places and animals and trees, dwelt a spirit which it was necessary to appease, from ancient times to today.

In ancient Egypt, people worshiped a multitude of spirits inferior to the divine who made up the court, giving glory to the gods.

In Mesopotamia, an incalculable number of spirits had a decisively personal character and exercised an influence on human affairs which was often considered conclusive.

In Persia two thousand years before Christ, before and after the reform of Zoroaster, belief in intermediate beings, both good and bad, was very much alive. The worst of these was Ahriman, "the evil spirit" par excellence, who was the arch rival of Ormazd, "the savior spirit." Ahriman bore a certain resemblance to the "prince of this world" of whom St. John speaks. "He too had at his service other inferior evil spirits who seemed like fallen gods transformed. The figure of one of them, *aeshma daeva* ["demon of wrath"] spontaneously calls to mind Asmodeus of the biblical book of Tobit."[1]

The cult of the guardian deities of nature was very much alive among the Greeks and Romans. There were those who saw to the smooth operation of the mills and others who — impudently — broke crockery; there were those who presided over the successful delivery of young sheep and others who brought a fever to the sick.

Belief in the existence of these "genies" was so widespread that it even entered into the works of the philosophers. Among these, Pythagoras went so far as to construct a system of metaphysics based on the existence of beings intermediate between the gods and men.[2]

As far as Plato is concerned, it is evident that the *daimon* is, for him, a personal being intermediate between divinity and humanity, strong enough to promote the progress of human beings along the right road.[3]

Aristotle knows of "beings beyond the heavens who are not subject to change or to strong desires and who eternally lead a wonderful life."[4] Each one of them is in charge of the movement of one of the heavens and is an intelligent intermediary between the "Immovable Mover and man, thus becoming an element in the explanation which Aristotle gives of the motion of the universe."[5]

Chrysippus, and along with him other Stoic philosophers, took account, in their system, of spiritual beings incapable of full

---

[1] M. Flick-Z. Alszeghy, *Il Creatore* ["The Creator"], Libreria Editrice Fiorentina, Florence, 1967, p. 521.

[2] Ibid., p. 522.

[3] Cf. *Symposium* 202.

[4] *De Coelo*, I, 1, c. 9.

[5] H. de Lubac, *Surnaturel* ["The Supernatural"], Paris, 1946, pp. 214-217.

freedom from suffering and divine felicity but who were nonetheless far superior to human beings. They were both good and bad. The latter were perhaps the cause of disasters and human iniquity.

It is therefore clear that from the very earliest times "the persuasion of the existence of personal beings inferior to the divinity and superior to men, has been universal. Not only, but it is part of the image of the universe."[6]

This universal belief constitutes an important factor in our rediscovery of the angels.

On the other hand, precisely because of this, it is good to be vigilant and attentive, focussing on certain aspects of the problem.

What are the reasons for this belief's being so widespread?

At one time people spoke of a primitive revelation handed down from generation to generation even outside the Hebrew people. And this is not an argument that can be simply stored away or dismissed.

Historians of religion are aware that often the divinities of one religion supplanted by another frequently don't disappear entirely but find a niche, at times, as beings subject to the higher gods while remaining themselves superior to human beings.

Then there is a reason of a philosophical nature. Above all in the Greek culture, the material world was regarded with a certain contempt when compared with the infinite transcendence of divinity. How can there be any contact, then, between the world and God? Here is the solution they found to the dilemma: to think of intermediary beings.

But Christian philosophy did away with this kind of reasoning by throwing light at one and the same time on the transcendence and the immanence of God: his having pre-existed and created the universe out of nothing, and his being

[6] M. Flick-Z. Alszeghy, op. cit., p. 524.

present everywhere as its cause and sustainer. His immanence was never so clearly manifested as in the Incarnation.

Finally, there is an argument of even greater weight in the development of these beliefs: the tendency of the human intellect to seek an explanation of various phenomena without having immediate recourse to the first cause.

When faced with misfortunes or sudden deaths, the natural course of things proves elusive. What can one think at such times? That God has intervened as the direct and immediate cause? Of course not.

Whether dealing with these unusual incidents or with precise and changeless laws, it seemed convincing to assert that a spirit might be behind them.

Genies or angels of streams and stars, of fevers and flowers, of births and deaths: these were the artisans of the exciting and at the same time dreadful vital drama in which we are immersed.[7]

Even with regard to one's own interior mystery — the experience of inexplicable forces — human beings have sought to explain them by positing the intervention of good and evil spirits.

So, at times projecting and personifying these good and evil forces in their own subconscious, people would think of good or evil genies, of angels or demons.

What weight should be given today to all of this? I think that a sane demythologization is an extremely positive thing.

In fact, too often in the past (and in certain socio-cultural classes even today) there has been the inclination to confuse the action of angels and demons with phenomena obtained through magic or an obscure kind of metaphysics.

Thus the morbid flowering of superstition has replaced the robust exuberance of the Christian belief in angels.

We have to make a bold but clean break with all these

[7] Ibid., p. 525.

superstitions without throwing out valid theological and even philosophical reasoning present in contemporary thought.

Regarding reasons of a theological nature, the assertions of M. Flick and Z. Alszeghy in their monumental work on the Creator are interesting: "The existence of purely spiritual beings makes the image of the universe — which appears so symmetrically put together by spirits, material beings and man, in whom matter and spirit are united — more harmonious."[8]

In the philosophical field, Jacques Maritain[9] and Henri Bergson both favor the existence of angels.

Bergson presents a very suggestive argument in this regard.

God created the universe urged on by love, thus entering into personal communication with his creatures.

But if only men existed, the majority of whom were deaf, indifferent and often rebellious to the Love which called out to them, we would be tempted to say: "Lord, you have failed because so few ever pay any attention to you."

On the contrary, if angels also existed, this persuasive call of God who is Love will regularly find a more adequate response. And our hearts as believers also find satisfaction in this.[10]

2. *The Eclipse of the Angels: Why and How*

In our day and age, one could talk about an eclipse of the angels. Not, obviously, in the sense that they had to beat a retreat, but because they are increasingly forgotten all about. Instead, it is urgent that they be spoken of, for that is the only

[8] Cf. Ibid., p. 525.

[9] J. Maritain, *Les degrés du savoir* ["The Degrees of Knowledge"], Paris, 1932, pp. 436-439.

[10] H. Bergson, *Les deux sources de la morale et de la religion* ["The Two Sources of Religion and Morality"] in *Oeuvres*, Paris, 1959, p. 1192.

way, in fact, to get rid of all prejudice, reserve, doubt and deceitful silence surrounding them, all of which amounts to a thorny hurdle that, on the level of a very widespread mentality, would hinder us from a serene penetration into the knowledge of this large part of creation.

What are the reasons behind this eclipse?

The first is to be sought in the philosophical currents of these last centuries. We are well aware of how rationalism and illuminism from the 17th and 18th centuries have exalted reason to the point of compelling everyone to genuflect before it and its "lights."

Distancing itself ever more from God, Western thought literally found itself bowing before an exasperated anthropocentrism.

If God becomes ever more sidelined and man plants himself at the center of everything, then his self-sufficiency can reach absurd limits.

It's enough to think of Jean-Paul Sartre who raved on about man as an "absolute freedom who invents Reason and the Good and who has no limit beyond himself."[11] Men like Sartre — and before him Marx, Nietzsche, and Freud — moved beyond the platform of the exaltation of the autonomy of man to an unreserved atheism.

Those who, while professing to believe in God, "associate the angels and demons with the personification of psychological realities and willingly see in them a mythical interpretation of reality to which psychoanalysis could provide the key"[12] are the heirs of that mentality.

The second reason for the above mentioned eclipse resides in a kind of euphoria which has grown up around scientific progress and the increasingly prestigious applications of technology.

---

[11] J.-P. Sartre, *Situations*, I, Paris, 1947, p. 334.

[12] J. Daniélou, *Gli angeli e la loro missione* ["The Angels and Their Mission"], Ed. Paoline, Pescara, 1957, p. 5.

In effect, within the space of a little more than a century, man has shot ahead of an evolution which brought him, for many reasons, to realize the biblical injunction to "subdue the earth."[13]

This euphoria surrounding positivist and agnostic scientism has already been surpassed in fact by men like Albert Einstein and J.C. Eccles who, precisely on account of their discoveries, were struck and amazed by the mystery of God.

However, even if some have had second thoughts about the possible consequences of a science divorced from faith in God (think, for example, of the harsh irony of a neutron bomb that destroys life but saves objects), the popular mentality is still contaminated by false assurances. It is this kind of outlook that has infected the thought of several theologians, among them the Protestant Rudolf Bultmann, who states: "One cannot use electric lights, the radio, and the modern instruments of medicine and chemistry in cases of illness and still believe in the world of spirits and the miracles of the New Testament."[14]

Another reason for this eclipse, which is also a typical manifestation of the disappearance of the angels from the world's horizon as it approaches the year 2000, is to be found in the mass media.

People today are "TV people" accustomed to contact reality indirectly through the media, a reality which is typically "shaped" by images,[15] not only on television but also in illustrated magazines, motion pictures and ads of every kind.

Manipulated by enormous economical and political powers which revolve around consumer cycles, the mass media (in

---

[13] Genesis 1:28.

[14] R. Bultmann, *Kerygma und Mythos*, I, Hamburg/Bergstadt, 1955, p. 18.

[15] By "contoured reality" is meant the fact that the "image" reproduces things in their total contours and surroundings. Discourse in words signifies concepts in an immediate fashion, whereas images convey meanings in a mediated fashion. I say, for example, that so-and-so is a good person and this is immediately understood. If I had to say the same thing in images, however, the thing would become much more complicated. Precisely because of its

a hidden and therefore more effective way!) influence the subconscious in ways that can be reduced to the single imperative: "Buy!"

So that you will buy and consume, I entertain you. Because you buy and consume, I provide work that is little more than robotic. So that you will buy and consume, I stimulate and shape your desires: all of them of a material nature only, within a setting that is wholly hedonistic and emotionally charged.

So that you will buy and consume, I, with increasing stealth, will silence your need for God and offer you in exchange an artificial paradise and a new paganism with idols of success, career, eroticism and the myths of prestige, an easy life and easy money, opulence and drugs, with seances and the pseudo liturgies of the sports arena, as well as prophecies from horoscopes and fortune-tellers.

Within this "world vision," obviously, there is no room for angels. And so, not only does silence fall upon them but derision as well.

From past, even if anthropomorphic, representations of them by artists of the calibre of Beato Angelico, Masolino da Panicale and others all of whom reflected a profound veneration for these beings of pure light, we have arrived at the banality of little chocolate angels and representations of them on wrapping paper; worse yet, at their caricature in certain songs or humorous vignettes in the newspapers like that of the astronaut who, not having captured anything else on the moon, returns to earth with a tiny angel... in a cage.

These seem to be the main reasons for a progressive obfuscation (often even to the complete disappearance of any

---

peculiar mode of communicating things, the image, if it is not "read" properly, tends not only to overwhelm, but in and of itself to contribute to an increasingly vulgar and widespread materialism. What exists is what I see; what I do not see does not exist. On the nature of the image, and on the semiological and psychosocial problems of the mass media, see N. Taddei, *Educazione all'immagine e con l'immagine* ["Education to and with Images"], Rome 1976.

mention in sermons or in religion classes) of the truth about the angels.

On the other hand, it is only right to observe that, in a climate of greater critical awareness of the true faith, beliefs permeated with mythical and superstitious elements progressively have been eliminated.

The judgment of the Church and of those theologians who, being true men of God, are also true theologians, is exacting, reserved, and prudent. As the Council taught, it is a good thing to go into the realities underlying the symbols of faith and to transpose them into our modern logical categories in order to "carefully search out the meaning which the sacred writers really had in mind."[16]

But the work of sifting out the perennial truths of the faith from some of the contingent historico-cultural elements in which they are found is a very different thing from simply reducing the angels to pure symbols or elements of archaic concepts and language. The fact of the matter is that angels are ever present not only in the Bible but throughout the patristic tradition, in the Magisterium of the Church, and in the liturgy.

To deny that angels exist would be like trying to deny the reality of the hearth simply because in modern homes heating methods are different from what they used to be in ancient times.

3. *The Angels Are Not Competitors of God*

It was not by chance that the theologian Karl Rahner wrote that the angels "are not competitors of God but rather his creatures."[17]

---

[16] Vatican Council II, Dogmatic Constitution on Divine Revelation, *Dei Verbum*, #12.

[17] K. Rahner, "Angeli," in *Dizionario teologico*, Italian Edition, Edited by G. Riva, Queriniana, Brescia, 1974, p. 117.

Down through the ages many have fallen into exaggerated cults in their regard.

In the earliest days of the Church, St. Paul deplored the fact that some preferred to venerate the angels rather than holding fast to Christ, "the Head, from whom the whole body [the Church], nourished and knit together... grows."[18]

The author of the Letter to the Hebrews, probably a contemporary of St. Paul and at least a benefactor of his doctrine, emphasized the centrality of the mystery of Christ and his supereminent grandeur before the angels: the Son "reflects the glory of God and bears the very stamp of his nature, upholding the universe by his word of power... [He is] so much superior to angels as the name he has obtained is more excellent than theirs."[19] Or again: "For it was not to angels that God subjected the world to come" but to him "for whom and by whom all things exist."[21]

Thus there is no question of a world of angels subsisting solely in and for itself. Nor is it a question of a dazzling maelstrom of pure light, unconcerned with God and belittling of Christ. This must be absolutely clear from the beginning because in the past there has been a certain mawkish or sentimental way of speaking about angels based on an unenlightened credulity which envisaged both heaven and earth as populated with sweet little "cherubs" all dressed in blue and as bright as neon lights.

In a manner inversely proportional to this kind of sentimentality, the heirs of our own materialistic and world-weary culture have called into question the very existence of any angels at all. And the weapons they use, as we have seen, are silence or

[18] Colossians 2:19.

[19] Hebrews 1:34.

[20] Hebrews 2:5.

[21] Hebrews 2:10.

ridicule and the pretentious pretext, on the part of certain theologians, of not wanting to create competitors with God.

So who, then, are the angels? And upon what is our belief in their existence based?

When we recite the Creed, the expression of a faith that goes back to Christ and to the apostles, we affirm our belief "in one God, the Father, the Almighty, maker of heaven and earth, and of all that is seen and unseen." Obviously among those things created by God which are "unseen" are to be found the angels. They originated as part of the creative inventiveness of an all-powerful Love when, as the Bible expresses it so poetically, "the morning stars sang together... [while God] laid the foundation of the earth."[22]

Merely to know that the angels exist and are part of this marvelous created universe, of which the center is Christ, has to be a major consolation and joy for us. By contrast, to enter into the narrow perspective of those who deny the existence of the angels in the name of a supposed greater grandeur and glory of God is actually to impoverish the very idea of a Creator.

God did not create the universe as a result of a series of petty geometrical calculations. Rather, he created an inexhaustible abundance of animals, vegetables, and minerals. There is the sparkle of lapis lazuli, and the perfect miniature corollas of flowers, incredibly small and aromatic. There is the trunk of the elephant and the tail of the squirrel, the little feathers of the redbreasted robin and the elegance and gravity of the flight of the eagle. There is an entire world out there which we can touch and see, and yet its many complexities nevertheless elude us, so varied are the species and the subspecies which compose it.

It is a world, in short, so full of beings and things that all of it often seems wasted on us. Who, for example, will ever contemplate the peaks of unclimbable mountains or the iridescence of

[22] Job 38:7, 4.

certain hidden quartzes? What about the inaccessible abysses of the oceans or the patterns of certain seaweed? Who will ever take in the songs of certain birds in the depths of certain forests?

Everywhere there are signs of a God stupendously prodigal in his creation.

In reflecting on ourselves as thinking beings, incarnate spirits who draw from our material existence the ways and means of acting yet who still remain finite and limited, we perceive ourselves to be the *summit* of creation. How, then, as reasonable beings can we reject out of hand the idea of the existence of beings who are purely spiritual?

It is precisely our reason which is comfortable with the thought that, in the scale of beings from minerals up to God who is Being or Love par excellence, the angels occupy a place which would be strangely empty without them: they occupy the place of created pure spirits.

Still, even if they surpass us in beauty and their dignity is so great as to enable them to enjoy the direct vision of God, it must yet be said that, in fact, *the Creator made the angels in view of our salvation!*

"For it is clear that he did not come to help the angels, but the descendants of Abraham."[23]

The author of the Letter to the Hebrews even went so far as to write: "Are not all angels spirits in the divine service, sent to serve for the sake of those who are to inherit salvation?"[24]

4. Identity of the Angels

"Spirits with a ministry" is one way the angelic identity might be defined.

The Hebrew word *"mal'ak,"* which means "angel," is de-

[23] Hebrews 2:16.

[24] Hebrews 1:14.

rived etymologically from the root "l'k," which means "to carry a message" or "to carry out a mission."[25]

The fact, moreover, that this terminology attributed to the angels should have had a pre-biblical origin is of some interest.

It should not disconcert us unduly to learn that the goddess Asherah, in the belief of the ancient Semitic peoples, had servants such as Rades and Amran who were "reflections of the glory of their Lord" and were esteemed as "angels" by these same ancient peoples.[26]

It is rather like discovering certain "seeds" of truth which, spread by the wind of the Spirit, took root in ancient cultures far away from the primary seedbed of Revelation.

Undoubtedly, "popular conceptions as well as oriental religious symbolism played a notable role in the representation of these beings."[27] What is really important, however, is not how the angels were represented but that they existed.

Religious symbolism is an interpretative filter of reality; it is a kind of language or way of speaking.

I can portray autumn colors, daybreak, or the enchantment of a twilight in many different ways and using many different modes of expression. I can depict them in a painting, with music, in prose, or in verse.

What counts is the reality of what I have in mind in my particular description.

And so it is with the angels: even though we may imagine them with wings, with multiple eyes, as young men dressed in white garments, or as young wayfarers — they nonetheless always remain pure spirits.

Scripture says nothing about the nature of angels, but speaks of them in terms of their "office" and of the functions

---

[25] *Dictionnaire de la Bible*, I, Supplement, Paris, 1928, p. 242.

[26] *Enciclopedia biblica illustrata*, I, Marietti, Turin, 1976, p. 65.

[27] A.M. Canopi, *Schede bibliche pastorali* ["Pastoral Biblical Forms"], EDB, Bologna, 1976, p. 14.

which we know that they have carried out — their roles of messengers, guardians, and "liturgists" (that is, of those given to the continuous praise of God in heaven).

In their invisible mode of being they are, of course, most mysterious. Nevertheless they truly do exist, and the pages of Scripture are replete with mention of them.

What is most worthwhile rediscovering about the angels, though, is the fact of their considerable influence upon the world and particularly of the world of the saved which is the Church.

Karl Rahner is entirely correct when he insists that we should not picture the angels to ourselves "on the basis of an anthropomorphic model which assumes the categories of space and time and conceives of them simply as a number of inconsequential spiritual beings deprived of materiality who, in the manner of a spiritualistic seance, act on the human and material world in accordance with their own whims, without having any real, substantial, permanent, and organic relationship with it."[28]

We must understand, as Erik Peterson writes, that man "is merely a part of creation and, for the most part, fulfills himself only in relationship with other beings — including angels and devils.

"It is important to realize that the angels relate not only to what man is at the moment but also to what he will become. Thus, it is truly in no way useless to try to understand who the angels are, for what they have to teach us about their own mode of being reveals something about the mode of being towards which we are in some sense tending.

"The angels are much more than mere personages in a poetic and popular drama. They live in the sphere of the Father, of Christ, and of the Holy Spirit, and yet they also live in our sphere! They represent a level of being one step above our own

[28] K. Rahner, "Angelologia," in *Dizionario teologico,* op. cit., p. 122.

and one degree more intense than ours to which, by means of love, we also can aspire."[29]

It is a fact that, in the very provisional character of our human condition in which what we shall be has not yet been revealed,[30] "if we do not make the effort to be like the angels who live in the presence of God, we shall most surely be like those spirits who have become separated from him, namely, the devils. This is the case because man can only exist by going beyond himself, thus moving towards either the angels or the demons."[31]

Here, even as I write, angels are present.

They will influence my spirit in a wholly beneficent way when, in a little while, they help dispose me to pray.

And if I send a thought to them in order to dialogue more intimately with those with whom I live, then I will emerge more easily from my isolation and succeed much better in communicating. Thus the daily effort to escape from egoism and move towards truth by loving others and growing together with them in Christ will not shatter into a thousand disappointments.

The angels are the messengers of God in what pertains to our salvation in Christ Jesus.

Certainly Christ is all: the keystone of the vault and the cornerstone of the building in everything that pertains both to our personal history and to the history of the world.

And the angels are Christ's servants and his intelligent emissaries sent to help us freely save ourselves.

---

[29] Erik Peterson, *Das Buch von den Engeln* ["The Book of the Angels"], Leipzig, 1935 (*La livre des Anges*, French translation of C. Champillon, Preface by Jean Daniélou, Bruges, 1955, pp. 93-94).

[30] Cf. 1 John 3:2.

[31] Peterson, op. cit., p. 95.

5. *The Angels and Cosmic Revelation*

Once again, Karl Rahner authoritatively asserts: "Today, when only too willingly it is considered entirely reasonable to believe in the existence of intelligent beings beyond the confines of this earth, given the enormous extent of the cosmos, man must not *a priori* reject the existence of the angels as unthinkable. These angels, however, should certainly not be considered as mythological additions to a celestial religion, but in the first place as the 'powers and virtues' of the cosmos."[32]

Our universe, which is now scrutinized through the lens of increasingly powerful telescopes, has been progressively revealed to our admiring eyes as considerably more vast than ever thought possible before. Thus, to believe in angels today is in no way anachronistic. Quite the contrary! If anything, it is to see more deeply into the true harmony of the cosmos.

Nevertheless, even in this fuller perspective, strict theological lucidity and precision remains an absolute requirement.

There are those who have pointed out how in our day science has often served as "a mythology for our times."[33] In the enthusiasm of learning that in the Milky Way alone there exist more than 10,000 stars similar to our sun, with probable planets revolving around some of them as hospitable to the development of life as this earth is, it has also been hypothesized that the angels could well be strange beings coming from even stranger planets.

In the same way, some seem to translate into another "myth for our times" that which has been said regarding the angels in the biblical books themselves; yet this testimony of Scripture really points to something else entirely.

[32] K. Rahner, "Angelologia," in op. cit., p. 121.

[33] Cf. C. Meyer, *Il Magistero su Angeli e demoni* ["The Magisterium on Angels and Demons"], in *Concilium*. 3, 1975, p. 102.

On this subject, the voice of Father Karl Rahner, already quoted several times, again seems to me to be not only authoritative, but also marvelously clarifying, when he says that angels "cannot be the subject of an experiment of the scientific type, that is, something empirical and quantitative, since such experiments must always be concerned by definition, whether objectively or subjectively, with the natural order."[34]

Let us therefore not wander afield by speaking of the angels in terms of the size and complexity of the physical universe, as if one day or another a space probe equipped with powerful enough instruments might finally succeed in verifying the existence of angels through the means available to science.

Rather, considering the enlarged mystery of the universe which is progressively verified, let us be stimulated to contemplate the grandeur of God and of all his creation as well.

Pausing a little and contemplating all this, as well as thinking of those purely spiritual creatures who are the angels, we can see a deeper harmony in all things, both visible and invisible. As for the visible, both the Fathers of the Church, and the particular theologian we have been quoting, do not hesitate to say that "it is reasonable to consider the natural order to be founded on and guided by such 'principalities and powers.'"[35]

Cosmic revelation (which St. Justin said was to be found in the works of those disciples of the Word who preceded the Incarnation of the Word, namely, Plato and Aristotle) always considered the angels invisible messengers of glad tidings.

When the ancient Chaldeans — to whom the Magi belonged — studied the stars and drew lessons from them that were supposed to guide peoples' lives and contribute to their

---

[34] K. Rahner, "Angelologia," in op. cit., p. 121.

[35] Ibid., p. 120.

wisdom, they were guided by the angels, according to some of the Fathers of the Church.[36]

Other Fathers maintained that everything true, good, and beautiful known to the pagans had been "given by the Providence of God through the ministry of the angels."[37]

There was, therefore, a complete theology of history which could not prescind from the existence of angels if it were itself to exist.

Extending our view back further into the history of primitive peoples, we always come upon just men trying to seek God.

They searched for God by studying the stars, by looking at created things, or by philosophizing. Sometimes they searched for him only by stumbling in the dark, feeling their way along as they went.

It was always the cosmic revelation providentially confided by God to the angels, though, which generally came through and was grasped by these just men, persuading them in their inner consciences of the goodness of God.

By contrast, it was the perversion of this same revelation — idolatry — which often came to be adopted to their own detriment by those who opened up their minds and hearts not to the angels of God, but to demons.

6. *The Angels and a Significant Cultural Mediation from the Past*

I would like to put on record and to underline here, even if briefly, what Pseudo-Dionysius had to say about the angels. Pseudo-Dionysius was an author of the fifth century A.D. who,

---

[36] In this regard, see what Jean Daniélou has written not only about the astral religion of the Chaldeans, but about that of some of the other ancient peoples, in "The Angels and Cosmic Religion" in op. cit., pp. 23-33.

[37] Ibid.

up until the time of the Protestant Reformation (16th century) was confused with Dionysius the Areopagite who was a disciple of St. Paul and whose conversion was mentioned in the Acts of the Apostles.

I want to speak about this author in particular since he represents one of the highest summits of patristic thought. Regarding his doctrine on the angels, it was so highly esteemed that St. Thomas Aquinas himself borrowed from Pseudo-Dionysius in his *Summa Theologica*.

Up until a few years ago, the most common popular account of the Church's doctrine on the angels was, in effect, a popularization based on the thought of Pseudo-Dionysius.

What must be underscored about him in his book on the angels, *The Celestial Hierarchy*, is his close adherence to sacred Scripture and to the great patristical tradition which had preceded him. However, he also stuck closely to the thought of Plato and even more to that of the Neoplatonists who came after Plotinus, especially Proclus. Finally, Pseudo-Dionysius definitely followed closely an earlier theologian, himself greatly influenced if not dependent upon the Neoplatonists; this theologian he called his "divine master," Hierotheos, whose writings he did not hesitate to characterize as a "second Scripture."[38]

The work of Pseudo-Dionysius is a substantial treatise which presents the angelic world as, in fact, a celestial hierarchy. Quite obviously the hierarchy in question is one in which the various ranks are based not upon power or on such other things as are typically found in purely human hierarchies, but rather upon sanctity and upon the sacred.

According to Dionysius, there are three distinct celestial hierarchies, each of which comprises three choirs.

In the first and highest of these hierarchies are to be found

---

[38] R. Rocques, "Introduction" to *Denys l'Aréopagite, La hiérarchie celeste*. Cerf, Paris, 1958, p. LXXXIII.

the Seraphim, the Cherubim, and the Thrones; in the second are to be found the Dominations, the Virtues, and the Powers; and in the third the Principalities, Archangels, and Angels. The highest level or degree is that of the hierarchy closest to God which, in hierarchical fashion, precisely, has an influence on the second level, as this second level has on the third, and so on, by means of a process of mediation and illumination.

The scholar René Rocques, in a masterly introduction to the work of Pseudo-Dionysius in the series *Sources Chretiennes* ["Christian Sources"], wrote as follows on this topic: "The nine angelic denominations, also in the theology which preceded Dionysius came from Sacred Scripture (the Old Testament and the Letters of St. Paul), while the notion of hierarchy and its division into triple choirs, as well as the laws which regulated its mediating functions, corresponded to opinions of Dionysius himself or those which had come from his master Hierotheos."[39]

What can we think today about this elaborate system of thought, the popularization of which was destined to have such good fortune as to be taken for the Church's own doctrine on the angels virtually up until our own day?

It appears quite evident to me that the great Dionysius has to be accorded the merit of having ranged over the broad horizons of God and his angelic creation with a very sharp eye and a heart full of love, paying careful attention to the revealed Word of God.

At the same time, it cannot be denied that Dionysius yielded to the seductive attraction of a cultural milieux of undoubted fascination, especially when he tried to reconcile certain biblical data with the kind of argumentation typical of the philosophical thought of that era, especially Neoplatonism.

It was no accident that the scholar already quoted, René Rocques, observed further: "The intention was obviously to

[39] Ibid., p. LXXXII.

reconcile wisdom and philosophical reflection with a revelation which belonged to an extra-rational order and to underline the harmony of the two orders, the order of knowledge and the order of divinization."[40]

Thus, as the Neoplatonist Proclus did not disdain the introduction of the superhuman into his philosophical order and made ample use of hierarchical and theandrical categories, so Dionysius, for his part, taking elements from Proclus through his own "divine master, Hierotheos," freely mixed philosophy with theology and attempted to reconcile both with revelation.

What does all this signify for us today, engaged as we are on a corrective reevaluation of the place of the angels in history? I believe it ought to give us the courage to get rid of all popular historical accretions, fuzzy ideas, and labored interpretations concerning the angels, in order to try to go to the real heart of the matter: what we need to adhere to as far as the angels are concerned is nothing other than what the Bible tells us about them and what sacred Tradition has therefore maintained about them down through the centuries (purified, of course, of outdated cultural infiltrations).

Thus, all of the elaborate hierarchical systems must also go, leaving the angelic universe as a living creation of Trinitarian Love which retains only those hierarchical denominations mentioned in Scripture.

What is especially important is that men should again become familiar with the angels. As Pavel Evdokimov has aptly written: "The incontestable evidence of demons functioning in our contemporary society calls for an especially privileged position for the angels and for the saints; for they too are just as real as the demons and just as real as other men."[41]

---

[40] Ibid., p. LXIV.

[41] P. Evdokimov, *Teologia della Bellezza* ["Theology of Beauty"]. Ed. Paoline, Alba, Italy, 1981, p. 80.

2

ANGELS IN THE LIFE OF ISRAEL

1. *Angels and the Bible*

I am well aware that to speak of the angels in Sacred Scripture in today's fevered theological climate is a bit like deliberately stirring up a sandstorm. One risks being submerged under the sheer weight of a variety of contradictory interpretations that are offered today.

On the other hand, why not seek in the Bible, precisely, the very solid certainty which pertains to the objectivity of the faith?

Thus, we shall willingly allow ourselves to be placed on our guard by those exegetes who talk about the "recasting of the narrative" regarding the angel in the Book of Tobit; or about all the "mythological elements" found in the description of the Cherubim in the Book of Ezekiel; or about the "symbolic visions" whose true significance is to be found beyond the symbol itself, as in the case of certain apocalyptic visions.

Nevertheless, even taking into account these incrustations and accretions on reality, which are an inescapable part of the human involvement in the composition of the Bible, we shall aim primarily at ascertaining revealed truth.

Amid the huge amount of dross, we shall concentrate on the single theme of the existence of the angels and their mission.

Also, we need to be clear about the reality of many modern studies on the subject.

In the thicket of every controversy on the angels, a dust cloud is thrown up whose ultimate origin is beyond doubt: namely, the all-pervasive scientific-positivistic mentality so prevalent in our culture.

Marranzini fairly punctually observed that this type of mentality "contains within itself an unconscious and almost instinctive *a priori* rejection of the angelic and demonic worlds which has prejudiced not a few critical and hermeneutical analyses of biblical texts today."[42]

When we read the various books of the Old Testament, we perceive that the angelology in them develops progressively.

In the most ancient period of the history of Israel, angels are present, but they do not stand out particularly.

When monotheism becomes the characteristic background of the narrative, however, a monotheism rooted in the descendants of Abraham, the sacred authors speak much more readily about the angels, even if, in describing them, they betray the influence of the civilizations with which they have come in contact.

There was a time when theologians tended to focus on this observation, deducing from it that the Church's doctrine on the subject of the angels was based on the Bible. End of argument.

Today much more is required. With the progress of modern historico-critical and philosophical methods, the student of the Bible must distinguish what the nucleus or kernel of the inspired discourse is in any given case; what belongs to the sacred author; what belongs to the social and cultural milieu of the day; and what pertains to the literary genre. Distinguishing all these things, in fact, constitutes an excellent way to proceed.

With regard to our present enterprise, what is important is

---

[42] A. Marranzini, "Angeli e Demoni," in *Dizionario teologico interdisciplinare,* Ed. Marietti, Turin, 1977, p. 351.

to learn what God teaches us about the angels in the inspired pages of the sacred book.

It seems to me important in this regard to bear in mind what the theologians M. Flick and Z. Alszeghy have said about all this.[43]

"Certainly it is of great interest to ask ourselves by what route the sacred author arrived at the affirmations he makes, and to what human influences he owes the opinions he expresses. Not everything expressed in the sacred books is the fruit of a special revelation.

"Sacred authors arrive at the convictions they express sometimes by making use of historical sources, sometimes by following a certain train of thought, and sometimes by having recourse to their own experiences and to those of others. What is always important to determine, though, is what an inspired author intended to affirm.

"Even if his affirmations arise out of human testimony that is perhaps tenuous, or from arguments that are themselves quite rudimentary, this does not diminish the value of the message.

"The value of the message, in fact, is not based upon the human affirmation considered in its origins, but rather upon the divine action which guarantees the truth of the affirmation.

"The correct way of evaluating biblical texts, then, is not merely to determine where the author obtained the doctrine he is affirming, but rather to examine closely to what extent the author wished to affirm it."

We come to realize in this way that there is an entire gamut in the numerous biblical texts which speak in some fashion of the angels: from those which speak of angels in a popular way intended to be edifying; to those which are used in a figurative sense to describe the grandeur or the Providence of God; to those which in fact speak of the authentic presence of angels.

There are, therefore, certain biblical texts which are truly

[43] M. Flick-Z. Alszeghy, op. cit., pp. 550-551.

"cardinal"—if I may use that term—to the argument regarding the existence of angels and their role in our regard.

When, for instance, Jesus said, "See that you do not despise one of these little ones; for I tell you that their angels in heaven continually look upon the face of my Father in heaven,"[44] he was surely not speaking in a figurative sense. On the contrary, he cited the angels as a reason for which the human person is always worthy of the greatest respect.

If Christ himself did not hesitate to refute or correct certain elements of the faith of his time (we need think only of his teaching about the Sabbath or the legalism of ablutions, and similar topics), why in the case of the angels should he not only not have denied their existence but went out of his way to affirm it?

With respect to the teachings of St. Paul and of the author of the Letter to the Hebrews, a denial of the existence of the angels would actually have reinforced their doctrine wherever they insisted on underlining the absolute supremacy of Christ over all "the principalities and powers."[45]

Since certain uneducated people of the time were inclined to put the angels ahead of the Savior, it would have made things much easier for these authors to deny out of hand the existence of these beings inferior to Christ than to maintain that "it was not to angels that God subjected the world to come" but rather to Christ.[46]

Instead, these authors not only reaffirm the existence of the angels but bring out their proper relationship with Christ and the Church, as, for example, when they state that the angels are all "spirits in the service of God, sent to serve for the sake of those who are to inherit salvation."[47]

What value should be given to the celestial liturgies de-

[44] Matthew 18:10.

[45] Colossians 1:15.

[46] Hebrews 2:5

[47] Hebrews 1:14.

scribed, for example, by Isaiah and Daniel? The former proclaimed: "Holy, holy, holy is the Lord of hosts; the whole earth is full of his glory."[48]

Or how should we interpret the presence of the angels in the Book of Revelation, where the triumph of the Lamb is described as celebrated by an immense multitude of angels?

Some, in fact, have wanted to read into this text especially solely a preoccupation with describing the infinite majesty of God by making use of popular forms of didactic narrative.

But this type of interpretation results in a major type of reductionism with respect to one thing that is very important to the dignity of the human being, namely, being called even in this life to join in the pure praise which the angels in heaven continually offer to God.

On this subject, a text from the Letter to the Hebrews carries great weight. This text reechoes the biblical theme of angelic praise, celebrating the greatness and superiority of the new people of the redeemed in most solemn terms and with divine inspiration: "You have come to Mount Zion and to the city of the living God, the heavenly Jerusalem, and to innumerable angels in festal gathering, and to the assembly of the firstborn who are enrolled in heaven..."[49]

It seems evident that if the praise of the angels were merely a literary ornament used to signify the fact that material creatures give praise to God, then it would not be a sign of greatness for the Church to associate herself with such praise.

When, however, it is affirmed that "the praise of God gives a meaning to the life of the angels in heaven and constitutes the ultimate end of the whole history of salvation here on the earth,"[50] then the significance and weight of the presence of the

---

[48] Isaiah 6:13; also Daniel 7:10.

[49] Hebrews 12:22-23.

[50] A. Marranzini, "Angeli e Demoni," in op. cit., p. 55.

angels in the enterprise of cosmic praise is not lost, and our own dignity in being associated with them is also augmented.

Having established these indispensable premises to our study, let us not linger any longer over these questions of an exegetical nature. In studying the presence of the angels in the Bible, we want to aim more at grasping the spiritual teaching inherent in their presence.

Breathing in this special angelic presence ourselves like a vital oxygen, let us allow our existence to be enriched and vivified by it.

In the Book of Job[51] as well as in the Psalms[52] the angels are called "sons of God."

Again in the Psalms as well as in other books, the angels are spoken of as "sons of the Most High,"[53] as "the mighty,"[54] and as "sentinels."[55]

The angels also constitute the "host" or "army" of the Lord,[56] or the "encampment" of God, as Jacob styled it when he met the angel in the course of his flight from the anger of his brother Esau.[57]

Indeed God himself is called "the Lord of hosts."[58]

This expression, taken in itself, may sound terribly cold and even evoke the image of a warrior God who makes himself strong with the strength of the armor bearers around him. In the biblical context charged with mystery, however, the expression rather effectively articulates the supereminent grandeur of a

[51] Job 1:6; 2:1; 38:7.

[52] Psalms 29:1.

[53] Psalms 89:7.

[54] Cf. Psalms 78:25.

[55] Daniel 4:10, 14, 20.

[56] 1 Kings 22:15; Psalms 148:2.

[57] Genesis 32:2.

[58] 1 Samuel 1:3, 11; Psalms 24:10; Jeremiah 7:3; 9:14.

Creator and Lord at whose merest nod or sign the angels respond with total assent and dedication.

"Thousands upon thousands were ministering to him, and myriads upon myriads attended him."[59] This expression indicates the futility of trying to calculate the number of these pure spirits; for there were unnumbered multitudes of them, all loved by God and created by him to govern, watch over, and protect men whose history, both before and after Christ, has in him its sole center of salvation.

Paul Claudel, a man whose stature as a believer was as eminent as it was as a literary man, once wrote: "From the angel of paradise to the one in the Book of Revelation, from the angel who appeared to Manoah to the one who enlightened Zechariah, from the angels who scourged Heliodorus to the one who guided the young Tobias, from the angel who consoled Hagar to the one who delivered Saint Peter, the entire sacred narration is replete with the presence of these awesome brothers and compassionate masters."[60]

The theologian Hans Urs von Balthasar put it this way: "They, who played an increasing role in the Old Testament as mediating beings and who, according to late Judaism and Paul, were actually mediators of the covenant on Mount Sinai, in the New Testament took on a secondary role, that of accompanying the life of the Son of God on earth.

"Their mediation between God and man is substantially no longer necessary since the Son has the Father always at his side[61] where he rests in the bosom of the Father,[62] and even acts in virtue of power received from the Father.[63] Nevertheless the

---

[59] Daniel 7:10.

[60] Quoted by G. Huber, *Il mio Angelo camminerà davanti a te* ["My Angel Will Go Before You"], Ancora, Rome, 1970, p. 37.

[61] Cf. John 8:16; 16:32.

[62] Cf. John 1:18.

[63] Cf. John 5:22.

angels can never be absent; in the first place, because they constitute such an integral part of the celestial glory of the Son of Man; and in the second place, and above all, because they are the ones who must make the social character of the Kingdom of heaven real — the Kingdom into which the entire cosmos is to be transformed."[64]

2. *Angels in the Lives of the Patriarchs*

From the first pages of the Book of Genesis, the presence of angels runs through the ambience in which Abraham, "our father in faith," was accustomed to move. Even if, sometimes, Abraham came into direct contact with God by means of interior illumination, often God communicated with him by means of his angels. The incident by the oaks of Mamre, where God appeared to Abraham's adoring piety, is especially famous: "And *the Lord* appeared to him by the oaks of Mamre, as he sat at the door of his tent in the heat of the day. He lifted up his eyes and looked, and behold *three men* stood in front of him. When he saw them, *he ran* from the tent door *to meet them,* and bowed himself to the earth, *and said, 'My Lord,* if I have found favor in your sight, do not pass by your servant'... *They said* to him, 'Where is Sarah your wife?' And he said, 'She is in the tent.' *The Lord said,* 'I will surely return to you in the spring, and Sarah your wife shall have a son.'"[65]

Was it God, one and Triune, who manifested himself to Abraham or were they angels announcing to him the great events tied to salvation history? And why the plural, "*they* said to him," followed later by "*the Lord* said"?

[64] Hans Urs von Balthasar, *Gloria: una estetica teologia, I, La Percezione della forma* ["Glory: An Aesthetic Theology, I, The Perception of Form"], Jaca Books, Milan, 1975, p. 633.

[65] Genesis 18:1-3; 9-10.

It is precisely here, at the very heart of this apparently contradictory text, that the biblical page literally palpitates with a sense of the transcendence of God and of the presence of the angels who were revealing him.

It is with very good reason that A.M. Canopi observes that "these messengers are not only the bearers of the Word of God but of his presence as well."[66]

Another scholar similarly comments that the use of angels as messengers constituted "a way of revealing the presence of God by rendering it something truly accessible to man, adapting the dazzling splendor of God's majesty to the weakness of our human condition."[67]

This was typical of the angel of Yahweh.

When Abraham lived to its climax the great drama of his radical assent of faith in God who appeared to be asking him to sacrifice his own firstborn son, it was the angel of the Lord who stayed his hand, reassuring him by saying: "Abraham, Abraham. Do not lay your hand on the lad or do anything to him; for now I know that you fear God, seeing you have not withheld your son, your only son, from me."[68]

The whole life of this chosen man flourished like a verdant field under the sun of God and his beneficent angelic interventions.

We need think only of the servant whom Abraham sent to seek a wife for his son in a non-heathen land, sending him off with these words: "The Lord, before whom I walk, will send his angel with you and prosper your way; and you shall take a wife for my son from my kindred and from my father's house."[69]

---

[66] A.M. Canopi, op. cit., p. 3.

[67] M. Balagué, "Angelo," in *Enciclopedia della Bibbia*, I, LDC, Turin, 1969, p. 466.

[68] Genesis 22:12.

[69] Genesis 24:40.

Beyond mere linguistic or literary considerations, here we are introduced into the splendor of revealed truth.

These words speak to us today and bring us consolation. For our life is not just a journey in some figurative or symbolical sense towards the land of God, our true eternal home, but in a very real way we traverse the pathways of this world inspired by the most diverse motives.

If to walk like Abraham — always in the presence of God — is the secret of interior unity and peace, then knowing also that an angel is always there escorting us means to understand where the nearest source of God's aid is to be found so that we may properly walk in his presence.

It is not by accident that Psalm 91 describes the mission of the angels as watching over every aspect of our lives: God "will give his angels charge of you to guard you in all your ways. On their hands they will bear you up, lest you dash your foot against a stone"(11-12).

The path trod by Jacob, another patriarch whom God enjoyed wrestling with in the course of a mysterious nocturnal challenge, was also a path marked by the constant presence of angels.

This man, to whom God gave the new name of Israel, as if to ratify with him the pact making him the founder of a people, had a dream which presaged the blessings of God which would come not upon him alone but also upon his extensive progeny out of which, as the sun of justice, would spring the Messiah himself.

"[He] dreamed that there was a ladder set up on earth, the top of it reaching all the way to heaven: and the angels of God were ascending and descending on it! And behold the Lord stood before him and said, 'I am the Lord, the God of Abraham your father and the God of Isaac; the land on which you lie I will give to you and to your descendants; your offspring shall be like the dust of the earth, and you shall spread abroad to the west and to the east and to the north and to the south; and all the families of the earth shall be blessed in you and in your descendants.'"[70]

There were many Fathers of the Church who saw in this mysterious ladder of Jacob an accurate representation of the Providence which God exercised over the world through the ministry of the angels.

Other Fathers of the Church liked to see in this incident a prefiguring of the Incarnation of the Word; a bridge between heaven and earth which the angels made use of in serving the Son of God and his mission.

Both of these interpretations can still validly serve our needs today.

What is important is not to forget that, in the economy of salvation, the angels occupy a definite place; one which shows forth the loving kindness of the Father and the light of Christ the Lord who is there to assist us in every situation and at every instant.

3. *Strong and Compassionate*

When the city of Sodom became a sink of iniquity, two angels appeared at its gates.

"When Lot saw them, he rose to meet them, and bowed down with his face to the ground."[71]

Lot invited them to come to his house and the two angels passed the night there while, outside, perverse inhabitants of the city called out demanding to have their will with these strangers; they almost broke the door down, but Lot held firm. Then the angels "struck with blindness the men who were at the door of the house, both great and small, so that they were unable to find the door."[72]

---

[70] Genesis 28:12-14.

[71] Genesis 19:1.

[72] Genesis 19:11.

Then, at dawn, "the angels urged Lot, saying,'Arise, take your wife and your two daughters who are here, or else you will be consumed in the punishment of the city.'"

After that, Sodom and Gomorrah were consumed in sulphur and flames because their gross sins had aroused the anger of the Lord.

Likewise, the story of Hagar, the slave girl by whom Abraham fathered Ishmael, persuades us of the firmness and the compassion of the angels, revealing at the same time the strength and love of God.

When this woman was on the point of fleeing the presence of Sarah, who had shown herself so hostile to her, the angel of God ordered her in severe tones to retrace her steps. The angel even promised her a son because, he said, "the Lord has paid heed to your affliction."[74]

Nevertheless there were still very painful days in store for her.

In the desert of Beersheba, Hagar, all alone with her little son, suffered the drama of abandonment: Abraham had banished her from his house forever.

And then the slave girl got lost in the desert.

In the depths of her desperation, she laid her baby under a bush and sat down some distance away so that she would not have to witness the child's death from thirst.

But "God heard the voice of the child; and an angel of God called to Hagar from heaven saying to her, 'What troubles you, Hagar? Fear not; for God has heard the voice of the lad where he is. Arise, lift up the boy and hold him fast by the hand; for I will make of him a great nation.'"[75]

Where the drama of an individual (or of a people), helpless

---

[73] Genesis 19:16.

[74] Genesis 16:11.

[75] Genesis 21:16.

and at the mercy of human power, is at its most critical — that is precisely where the compassionate goodness of God is manifested most plentifully through the intervention of the angels.

We need think only of the Persian king Darius who, acting under pressure from his subaltern satraps, had Daniel the prophet thrown into the lions' den.

In spite of the king's order that beyond his own person no other should be adored as god, Daniel went right on sending his prayers aloft to Yahweh, the living God. When Darius wished to ascertain what had befallen this Jew whom at bottom he esteemed and loved, he heard the following with his own ears from the depths of the lions' den:

"My God sent his angel and shut the lions' mouths, and they have not hurt me, because I was found blameless before him; and also before you, O king, I have done no wrong."[76]

Nebuchadnezzar was another king who had to be convinced of the grandeur and goodness of the true God through an intervention of angels acting to protect the young men he had had thrown into the fiery furnace.

Shadrach, Meschach, and Abednego had refused to join in the formal worship of a statue representing the king.

However, the flames destined to burn them consumed instead the Chaldeans who had ignited this sinister fire.

The king himself, bending down to see what had taken place within the fiery furnace, declared: "But I see four men unbound, walking in the middle of the fire, and they are not hurt; and the fourth has the appearance of a god."[77]

And when the three young men emerged unharmed from the furnace, Nebuchadnezzar himself praised God in these terms: "Blessed be the God of Shadrach, Meschach, and Abednego, who has sent his angel and delivered his servants

[76] Daniel 6:22.

[77] Daniel 3:25.

who trusted in him and set at naught the king's command and yielded up their bodies rather than serve and worship any god except their own God."[78]

Wherever innocence is most oppressed and trampled upon is precisely where the angels are likely to intervene.

But also wherever correction or punishment is called for, the angels are likewise apt to be present. They are like the warm bright sun of the month of May or the fierce power and force of the hurricane. They represent the two characteristic faces of the heavens at one and the same time; they are either suffused with sunlight or dark with menacing clouds; in either case the help they send down upon the earth is always beneficial.

But every time it is God alone, in Christ the Lord, who represents our heavenly salvation.

4. *Towards Liberation*

The biblical Book of Exodus, which narrates the departure of the chosen people from their slavery in Egypt, is the great epic prefiguration of our liberation from slavery to sin effected by Jesus and his paschal mystery. It is significant that when he presented the Law to Moses as a standard which the people had to follow in order to attain to liberty and justice, God specified the following: "Behold, I am going to send an angel before you to guard you on the way and to bring you to the place which I have prepared. Give heed to him and listen to his voice; do not rebel against him, for he will not pardon your transgression; for my name is in him. But if you harken attentively to his voice and do all that I say, then I will be an enemy to your enemies and an adversary to your foes. When my angel goes before you and brings you to the Amorites, the Hittites, the Perizzites, and the

[78] Daniel 3:28.

Canaanites... you shall not bow down to their gods, nor worship them."[79]

In the Bible its name is equivalent to the thing. The very power of the Lord, therefore, is present in his angel.

In his angels all the strength and tenderness with which God guards and guides his people is made manifest.

The presence and light of the angel reveals the august presence of the one and transcendent God so totally different from the numerous divinities of the peoples with whom, because of wars or their travels, God's people came into continual contact.

Whether it is a question of an entire people, or simply of single persons, the Lord intervenes by sending his angels in order that the difficult road to liberation may be traversed successfully.

Terrible and splendid at the same time, an angel, sword unsheathed, stood in the way and prevented Balaam's ass from going down the road to perdition.

Balaam, the Babylonian soothsayer engaged by Balak, an enemy of Israel, seemed to vacillate; he wasn't able to remain steadfast in his decision not to accept "silver nor gold" from the one who wanted him to curse Israel. And so, not once or twice but three times an angel stood in his way and prevented Balaam from passing.

Balaam struggled to understand, he agonized over it, and he got very angry at his ass for turning aside at the sight of the angel. In the end, however, he was made aware like a "man whose eyes are opened,"[80] and finally had the courage to reply to whoever might want him to do otherwise: "What the Lord says, that is what I will say." His tongue was loosened only that he might bless, not curse, Israel.

---

[79] Exodus 23:20-24.

[80] Numbers 24:3.

Even in the case of mysterious magical forces in the hands of diviners, it is still God who prevails. His goal is freedom. And the angels are his instruments for achieving it.

Again it was an angel who in the name of God reproved the people for getting caught up in the idolatrous cults of the peoples with whom they came into contact: "Why have you done this? So now I say, I will not drive them out before you; but they shall become adversaries to you, and their gods shall be a snare to you."[81]

At times the angel of the Lord actually became an executioner.

It was in the name of God that angels opposed those who were creating obstacles in the way of God's plan of salvation.

"That very night the angel of the Lord went forth, and slew a hundred and eighty-five thousand in the camp of the Assyrians, and when morning dawned, behold there were all the dead bodies."[82]

On the path to freedom, the prophets played an especially important role: they announced, in fact, what God wanted to have carried out in order that his plan of salvation culminating in the Incarnation of the Word might be realized.

Precisely because they were more closely associated with the work of God, these men had to undergo tremendous opposition, fight many battles, suffer much pain and fatigue. They would not have been up to it had the Lord not sustained them.

And it was often by means of the angels that the Lord came to their aid.

Typical of the kind of interventions made — which reveal something very paternal and at the same time very maternal in the sensitivity of God — were those related to Elijah.

When this man of God firmly opposed the priests of Baal, challenging them on Mount Carmel, he ran up against Queen

[81] Judges 2:23.

[82] 2 Kings 19:35.

Jezebel who threatened him with death. Worn out from a long flight into the desert, he longed to die, pouring out his heart in this very human prayer: "It is enough. Take my life now, O Lord...."

"Then he lay down under a broom tree and fell asleep. Suddenly, an angel touched him and said to him: 'Arise and eat.' He looked around and, behold, there at his head was a cake baked on hot stones and a jug of water. So he ate and drank, and lay down again. The angel of the Lord came again a second time, and touched him, saying, 'Get up and eat, otherwise the journey will be too much for you.' He got up, ate and drank, and went in the strength of that food forty days and forty nights to Horeb, the mount of God."[83]

It was on Mount Horeb that Elijah experienced in an ineffable way the mysterious presence of God, as had the people of God on the path to freedom, and as we do today on the road to salvation. The obstacles, then and now, are idols and their priests — different from what they once were, but in some ways even more attractive and enticing: money, things, comfort, an easy life. The mass media are the priests who keep these things before our eyes and serve as mediators between them and us.

In the very difficult task of swimming against the current, there arises at times for us, as there did for Elijah, a certain sense of tedium, fatigue, and even a desperate longing for death.

To endure in the spirit of the Word of God — "For freedom Christ has set us free,"[84] "For [we] were called to freedom,"[85] "Walk by the Spirit"[86] — the intervention of the angels on our behalf is in no way superfluous.

Within a lifestyle where freedom from the agnostic-materialistic mentality of our day and age is desired and pursued, the

---

[83] 1 Kings 19:48.

[84] Galatians 5:1.

[85] Galatians 5:13.

[86] Galatians 5:16.

angels help us by pointing us towards Christ, the Word of Life; towards Christ, the Eucharistic Bread.

If we are to remain on the path that leads to salvation, it is important to know how to profit from the help that the angels are able to give.

5. *The Greater the Consciousness of the One God, the Greater the Awareness of the Angels*

Israel lived out its epic conquest of the promised land, experiencing all the ups and downs of a people whose history, in the end, is symbolic of our own.

This history was comprised of an intricately woven complex of events. The basic thread running through it all was the sovereign fidelity of God and the recurrent infidelity of man.

The immediate consequences of these sins of infidelity were suffering, the regression of a religiosity which tended to become defiled with idolatry, and the long period of exile endured in Babylon.

As the Psalmist sang: "By the waters of Babylon, there we sat down and wept, when we remembered Zion. On the willows there we hung our lyres."[87] However, it was precisely during this exile of painful purification that Israel, confronted by polytheistic oppressors, acquired a deeper appreciation of the oneness and the transcendence of God.

It is an interesting fact that, especially during and after the exile, "after the monotheism of the Hebrews was thoroughly established, the angels came on the scene in greater numbers than ever, offering a service of aid and protection to the chosen people; this people, however, never failed to perceive the creatureliness of these beings."[88]

---

[87] Psalms 137:12.

[88] A. Marranzini, "Angeli e Demoni," in op. cit., p. 352.

And in this same period, it also became a question not merely of angels but of Cherubim, Seraphim, and Archangels.

"O Lord the God of Israel, who are enthroned above the Cherubim, you are God, you alone, of all the kingdoms of the earth."[89] Thus prayed Hezekiah, the king of Judah.

This, however, was not the only time that these spirits, given to the adoration of the thrice holy God, were singled out.[90] The Old Testament pictured them around the throne of majesty and glory.

It was the Cherubim who guarded the entrance of the terrestrial paradise. Impressive figures of these Cherubim were described by Ezekiel as surrounding God when he manifested himself in all his tremendous majesty in a mysterious "whirlwind of fire."[91]

The prophet saw how "each went straight forward; wherever the Spirit would go, they went, without turning as they went."[92]

These beings with many eyes moving solely under the impetus of the Spirit represent a mode of being fully alive for God: for them to contemplate and praise him is itself to live.

In their mode of being there is something that should also bring us back today to our contemplative roots which need to be revitalized from time to time if we are truly to remain ourselves.

It is not by accident that in the liturgy of the Eastern Church, prior to the offertory of the Mass, the *Cherubikon* is sung. It is a hymn which includes the following words: "We who mystically represent the Cherubim and sing the hymn thrice holy to the life-giving Trinity now put aside all worldly preoccupations in order to welcome the invisible King of the universe escorted by the angelic hosts."

---

[89] 2 Kings 19:15.

[90] Cf. 1 Samuel 4:4; 2 Samuel 6:2; 22:10.

[91] Ezekiel 1:1-10.

[92] Ezekiel 1:13.

The Seraphim appear in the great vision of Isaiah when he was caught up in trying to express in human words the ineffable majesty of God, sovereign of immense glory.

The ecstatic eyes of the prophet saw that each one of the Seraphim "had six wings: with two he covered his face, and with two he covered his feet, and with two he flew. And one called to another and said: 'Holy, holy, holy is the Lord of hosts; the whole earth is full of his glory.'"[93]

It is not enough simply to note that the portrayal of the wings constitutes an element borrowed from the Babylonians. We need to remind ourselves of the patristic tradition which attributed to this symbolic feature the idea of the promptness with which the messengers of God are absolutely available and submissive to God's every wish.

As for the Seraphim, it is noteworthy that their very name is related to the words for fire and lightning.[94]

We read in the profoundly mystical experience of the vocation of Isaiah that one of the Seraphim came to him, "having in his hand a burning coal which he had taken with tongs from the altar. And he touched my mouth, and said: 'Behold, this has touched your lips; your guilt is taken away, and your sins forgiven.'"[95]

Since Isaiah was being called to proclaim the Word of God, he had to be purified with respect to whatever of a sinful nature had passed his lips.

And it was through the instrumentality of one of the Seraphim that God brought about this urgent purification. Pseudo-Dionysius, who has already been quoted, made a special point of underscoring this purifying office of the Seraphim, which he also plainly said applied to us.

---

[93] Isaiah 6:23.

[94] Cf. L.A. Schökel in *La Bibbia: Parola di Dio scritta per noi* ["The Bible: Word of God Written for Us"], II, Marietti, Turin, 1980, p. 632, n. 2.

[95] Isaiah 6:67.

Examining in depth this aspect of patristic thought, Jean Daniélou observed: "The purifying operations come entirely from God as their unique source, but the principal ministers are the Seraphim."[96]

It is a fact that we, though occasionally guilty of the sin of not speaking enough, are often even more guilty of the sin of saying too much in a society which runs off at the mouth more than any other. Thus, while our hearts need to be purified, our tongues likewise need to be cleansed.

We need to be purified of words which cut like swords or pierce like pins; malevolent words or flattering ones; bitter words of protest or complaint; perfidious and calumnious words; words aggressive with impatience; lying, ambitious, and vain words; words of egotistical self-interest which reflect a narcissistic contemplation of one's own self; mocking, railing words, and arrogant ones; fatuous, stupid words and all kinds of words which lack the salt of evangelical wisdom, and most especially, love.

Too many such words issue from mouths without having been nourished in hearts truly open to God and to the message of his Word.

"Anyone who makes no mistakes in what he says," St. James tells us, "is a perfect man, able to keep his whole body in check as well."[97] He adds: "The tongue is a fire... setting ablaze the cycle of nature, and set on fire itself by hell."[98]

It is well, therefore, that purification should come, even if it is painful.

God brings it about in us through the instrumentality of the Seraphim, angels of the purest fire.

By means of this purification, we become capable of both

---

[96] J. Daniélou, op. cit., p. 107.

[97] James 3:2.

[98] James 3:6.

silence and speech: a silence indispensable in the service of evangelical salt and light, and characterized especially by the truth of our words.

6. *The Angels: Revealers of the Strength of God*

"The angel of the Lord encamps around those who fear him, and delivers them."[99]

This aspect of the strength of God manifested by the angels finds expression more than once in the books of the Bible which tell the story of the consolidation of the Hebrew people in spite of their opponents.

During the time of Antiochus Eupator (164-162 B.C.), one of the sovereigns who succeeded Alexander the Great at a moment of great conflict between Judaism and Hellenism, a man by the name of Lysias rose to great power. He not only wanted to take over Jerusalem and burden the Temple with taxes but even to "put the high priesthood up for sale every year."[100]

The sacred text describes this Lysias as follows: "He took no account whatever of the power of God, but was elated with his ten thousands of infantry, and his thousands of cavalry, and his eighty elephants."[101]

Against the challenge of this kind of self-sufficiency so typical also of modern man was the cry of those led by Maccabeus, who had involved the whole people in the defense effort. They prayed to God, asking that he send his angel; at the same time, they risked "their lives... to aid their brethren" who were being besieged in Jerusalem.

"While they were still near Jerusalem, a horseman ap-

[99] Psalms 34:7.

[100] 2 Maccabees 11:3.

[101] 2 Maccabees 11:4.

peared at their head, clothed in white and brandishing weapons of gold."[102] As a result, the spirits of the men of Maccabeus revived and they fought with great courage.

This brought about the defeat of Lysias.

What the sacred writer wanted to emphasize here was how God is on the side of those who have confidence in him and make room for his salvific work.

There is no comparison between the powers of the earth and those of heaven.

For the sacred writer, it was a typical practice to make use of the literary genre in vogue and to describe the intervening angel as wearing white and brandishing weapons of gold.

What counts for us, however, is to understand that God does intervene to help us if we will call upon him for such help.

God can provide that aid in very many ways, often by sending his angels.

Thus the courage to believe, which is the strength of Christ himself intervening in our lives, is reinvigorated because of the existence of the angels.

Regarding "angelology," Karl Rahner has aptly observed: "This subject allows man to understand an element of the time in which he lives by virtue of his faith-decision and *it prevents him from reducing its dimensions*. Man finds that he lives in a community of salvation or perdition that extends beyond humanity itself."[103]

Sometimes as a result of ignorance which channels the naturally religious impulses of man towards superstition, but sometimes also by reason of a prideful propensity to rationalize the data of faith, the faith itself can become incredibly impoverished.

By contrast, the wider the horizons encompassed by our

---

[102] 2 Maccabees 11:8.

[103] K. Rahner, "Angelologia," in op. cit., p. 122.

belief, the more intense becomes in us the thirst for the living God, revealing his boundless and unfathomable mystery.

And it is only to our loving thirst that God gives himself with the Love that is the foretaste of eternal life.

7. Michael the Archangel Against Satan

As we have seen, the more the transcendence of the one God was affirmed in Israel in the face of the idolatry in which the neighboring peoples were drowning, the more the angels came into the picture and were active.

Indeed, several angels with proper names and characteristic functions emerged at this time: Michael, Gabriel, Raphael, and the group of "seven holy angels who present the prayers of the saints and enter into the presence of the glory of the Holy One."[104]

In the apocryphal books, the names of other angels appear: Uriel, Raguel, Sariel, and Fanuel.[105]

For our purposes, though, it suffices to look at the three Archangels named here; they alone are mentioned in scriptural texts which the Church recognizes as inspired.

Michael, whose particular authority was underlined by the prophet Daniel, is well-known. Daniel styled him "one of the chief princes,"[106] or "your prince."[107] In some ways, he was the first humble or self-effacing creature in history. The name "Michael" signifies "Who is like God."

As we have already had occasion to note, biblically speaking, a name was always equivalent to the thing or being it designated.

---

[104] Tobit 12:15; cf. Daniel 10:13; Zechariah 4:10.

[105] Cf. M. Balagué, "Angelo," in op. cit., p. 466.

[106] Daniel 10:3.

[107] Daniel 10:21.

Even extra-biblical Jewish angelology gives prominence to the figure of Michael, not only as protector of the Jewish people,[108] but also as a compassionate defender during various trials,[109] and also as a depository of the secrets of divine Providence and a guide to heaven for souls.[110]

The famous Qumran community lived in an awareness of a dramatic opposition between light and darkness. It was not a matter of abstract categories to them, but of real opposing groups or forces. There were angels of light and those of darkness; the former were intent upon helping men, impelled to this by God; the latter tempted men to evil. Preeminent among the former was Michael.[111]

A liturgical text going back to the 10th century contains the following invocation: "Lord Jesus Christ, King of glory, free the souls of all the faithful departed from the pains of hell and from the deep abyss. Free them from the jaws of the lion, that they may not fall prey to Hades and languish in darkness, but rather let St. Michael the standard-bearer guide them into the holy light which you promised one day to Abraham and his descendants."[112]

Such interventions of the angels, especially of St. Michael, in favor of those who have already completed their earthly life and need to be borne to the bosom of God, serve to make us solicitous about the mystery of the next world.

Having passed beyond death, will we still be the object of Satan's avid striving for our souls? Is it not true that immediately after death the irrevocable judgment by which we will be saved or damned forever takes place? Since we are so conditioned by the categories of "time" and "space," we cannot really imagine

[108] Cf. Enoch 20:5.

[109] Cf. Enoch 40:9; 68:2.

[110] Cf. Enoch 61:3.

[111] Cf. Qumran 17:6.

[112] Cited in M. Flick-Z. Alszeghy, op. cit., p. 716.

the "how" of what will take place immediately after death. Nevertheless we can be consoled by these indications as we pray along with the Roman Ritual commending the souls of the departed to God: "May the angels lead you into paradise; may the martyrs come to welcome you and take you to the holy city, the new and eternal Jerusalem."

That St. Michael the Archangel, especially, was thought to be the angel who defended the newly deceased from the final assaults of Satan is something we can gather from a New Testament text, namely, the Letter of Jude: "But the Archangel Michael, contending with the devil in a dispute over the body of Moses, did not presume to pass a reviling judgment on him, but said, 'The Lord rebuke you.'"[113]

Some modern exegetes are not prepared to accept that the sacred author intended in this text to commit the authority of the revealed Word of God to an objective affirmation that this "altercation" between Michael and Satan actually took place.

In the same Letter of Jude, however, we read: "The angels who did not maintain their own dignity but deserted their proper place have been kept by him in eternal chains in the nether gloom until the judgment of the great day."[114] It is held that the sacred text here really alludes to the sin of the fallen angels.

There is greater evidence for this view if we consider what St. Peter also wrote on the same subject: "God did not spare the angels when they sinned, but cast them into hell and confined them in the pits of Tartarus to be kept until the judgment."[115]

The victory of the forces of Michael over those of the rebel angels was vividly described in the Book of Revelation: "Now war broke out in heaven. Michael and his angels fought against the dragon. The dragon and his angels fought back, but they

[113] Jude 9.
[114] Jude 6.
[115] 2 Peter 2:4.

were defeated and there was no longer any place for them in heaven. The great dragon, that ancient serpent, who is called the Devil and Satan, the deceiver of the whole world, was thrown down to the earth, and his angels were thrown down with him."[116]

At the center of the great symbolic description of the eschatological triumph of Christ over the forces of evil, the presence here of Michael and the good angels fighting against Satan and his wicked angels is very powerful indeed.

Modern exegetes, attracted to the central Christological message, often try to dissuade us today from regarding these verses as actually descriptive of the sin which transformed some angels into demons although they generally emphasize the fact that the mention of the dragon does indeed refer to Satan.

Thus it is worthwhile to pause for a moment to look further at this being who in late Judaism was called Satan, Belial or Beliar, Beelzebub, or the Devil.

His dark presence is affirmed to such a degree in both the Old and the New Testaments that to try to deny it by interpreting it as something merely symbolic, or as the personification of the obscure evil found in the world and shaped by the culture of those times, would be seriously to distort the very message of Christ himself.

The Savior's way of acting would be totally inexplicable were Jesus not really convinced of the reality of Satan.

One reacts also, and justly so, against the too credulous type of faith which, especially in certain socio-cultural strata, is little more than superstition which initially inspires fear, then skepticism and finally total indifference.

With serious theologians one must distinguish accurately between literary trappings, philosophical speculations and contingent elements belonging to historical and cultural circumstances and what the sources of the faith truly affirm. Only these

[116] Revelation 12:79.

are valid for all time. It is nevertheless still necessary to guard against rash affirmations which would go so far as to declare that demons are really "nothing,"[117] or to imagine that their existence had somehow been "liquidated" by the advent of more recent affirmations of the faith.[118]

In the end, all the vacillation, perplexity, and even outright denial regarding the existence of those whom Pope Paul VI did not hesitate to call "living, spiritual, corrupted, and corrupting beings"[119] reveal a very important aspect of Satan's own strategy to promote disbelief in his own existence today as never before.

In fact, as C.S. Lewis well knew and was able to express so persuasively in his famous book *The Screwtape Letters*,[120] nothing is more favorable to Satan's successful operations than the conviction that Satan is nothing but an imaginary holdover from medieval times, an obscurantist and even ridiculous figment of the religious imagination.

However, even a correct view of the real existence of Satan and his legions must still be understood strictly within the context of the absolute centrality of Christ and the entire economy of salvation to be obtained in and through him.

That a part of the angels led by Lucifer rebelled against God out of pride, being unable to tolerate the inscrutable design of the Father who so loved the world that he gave his only Son to become a man and be put to death for man's salvation, remains theologically valid.

---

[117] Cf. E. Schillebeeckx, "I demoni sono dei 'niente'" ["Demons are 'Nothings'"], in *Concilium*, XI (1975) n. 3, pp. 17-18; 21-33.

[118] H. Haag, *Abschied vom Teufel* ["Farewell to the Devil"], Einsiedeln, 1969 (Translated into Italian with the addition of a question mark in the title to avoid an otherwise only too well-justified negative reaction: *La liquidazione del diavolo?* Brescia, 1970.

[119] Pope Paul VI, "*Insegnamenti*" ["Teachings"], X, Vatican City, 1973, p. 1169.

[120] C.S. Lewis, *Lettere a Berlicche* ["The Screwtape Letters"], Mondadori, Milan, 1980.

To realize that there are such personal forces operating in the world, opposing with highly intelligent strategies the plan of God, is to realize at the same time how much greater the definitive victory is which God has won not only for the world but for ourselves as well.

What, then, is driving this prince of darkness and those angels who joined him in the rebellion against God at the beginning of creation?

Fundamentally, his objective is to distract our attention away from the solar light of Christ our Savior and to focus it upon illusory "lights" which only momentarily satisfy our desire for happiness, casting us down afterwards into the darkest disappointment.

It is while we are in such a state of distress that Satan then dangles before us the bait of despair, hoping thereby to transform us into his image and likeness for he is the spirit of desperation par excellence.

It was for this reason that St. Peter exhorted us: "Be sober, be watchful. Your adversary the devil prowls around like a roaring lion, seeking someone to devour. Resist him, solid in your faith."[121]

To be aware of the fact that Satan exists and is highly astute and capable is not the whole story, of course, although it is a good beginning if one wishes to avoid falling into one of his traps.

It is also necessary, however, to understand his strategy and tactics, which are those of all the demons, his companions in iniquity.

"Devils never work in general and in the abstract; they always have recourse to individual strategies, adapting them to the case at hand.

"They attack their victims where they are weakest or through centers of their greatest interest. With consummate

[121] 1 Peter 5:8.

ability and great tact they proceed gradually towards their goals, never skipping any steps."[122]

Creatures of division and dispersion, the demons try to tempt us especially in what regards the two great commandments of love, since this is where our inner forces are most concentrated.

Knowing that, without the love of God, all our efforts to love our fellow human beings will be in vain, their most congenial tactic is to impede our contact with God by stressing the boredom and uselessness of prayer.

St. Vincent de Paul expressed this very clearly when he wrote: "The devil does everything possible to impede us from praying, for he knows very well that, if he can succeed in filling us with frivolous thoughts, he will be in charge of us for the rest of the day."[123]

It is precisely when we become more aware of the action of Satan, both in our personal lives and in the world at large, that we have enlightened recourse to St. Michael the Archangel, strong in his transluminous humility.

Realistic and vigilant, yet not overcome by fear or gloom, we believe that there is much that Satan can do; we likewise know that he cannot overwhelm us totally either. Our free consent alone to good or evil is decisive in the question of our salvation or perdition.

It is our own consent that enables us to appeal to powers much stronger than Satan. Mary, "the woman clothed with the sun," who from the beginning was to "crush the ancient serpent's head," is our most powerful ally in the battle against Satan. She is like the dawn dispelling the perpetual darkness of the Evil One.

---

[122] G. Huber, op. cit., p. 84.

[123] St. Vincent de Paul, "*Entretiens aux Filles de la Charité*" ["Conversations with Daughters of Charity"], in *Correspondence, Entretiens, Documents*, IX, Paris, 1920-25, p. 32.

"I am Gabriel. I stand in the presence of God; and was sent to speak to you and to bring you this good news. But now, because you did not believe my words, which will be fulfilled in their time, you will be silent and unable to speak until the day that these things come to pass."[131]

In a society as markedly materialistic as our own, faith was, for many at that time, the last thing to which they wanted to commit their countless problems, delusions, and uncertainties.

Practically speaking, faith is considered a concession made from the height of presumptuous reason to the mystery which, like it or not, we sense surrounds us.

Gabriel, however, made it very clear that faith is something else.

Faith means to trust completely in God: in his plan, in his Word, in his wishes. These things are to be measured on the scale of God's infinite love and not on the scale of our own limited logic.

When, in the fullness of time, the Word of God became man, Gabriel was again involved.

On an otherwise very ordinary day, Gabriel presented himself to Mary of Nazareth. "In the sixth month the Angel Gabriel was sent from God to a city of Galilee called Nazareth, to a virgin betrothed to a man named Joseph, of the house of David; and the virgin's name was Mary. And he came to her and said, 'Hail, full of grace, the Lord is with you.' She was perplexed by this saying, and wondered what sort of greeting this might be. Then the Angel said to her, 'Do not be afraid, Mary, for you have found favor with God. And behold you will conceive in your womb and bear a son, and you shall name him Jesus."[132]

Mary did not take refuge in doubts; she was merely troubled.

---

[131] Luke 1:19-20.

[132] Luke 1:26-33.

In her life, as in any other, such an encounter with the supernatural was totally unprecedented.

She replied with a very human question, "How can this be since I have not known a man?"[133]

Gabriel did not hesitate to reveal God's secret.

"The Holy Spirit will come upon you, and the power of the Most High will overshadow you; therefore the child to be born will be called holy, the Son of God."[134]

Thereupon the angel offered as his credentials from the Lord to this maiden of Nazareth, the news that life was rekindled in the sterile womb of Elizabeth.

"This is the sixth month for her who was called barren."[135]

Then Gabriel focused the entire discourse with an observation more illuminating than a sudden flash of summer lightning on a star-spangled night: "Nothing is impossible for God."[136]

Mary's "yes," which grafted God's salvation onto the heart of the world, immediately "took." And it came about because of her certainty that it would indeed all come to pass just as the angel said.

In the end, when her elder cousin Elizabeth said, "You are blessed because you have believed,"[137] and she herself sang: "My soul magnifies the Lord... henceforth all generations will call me blessed,"[138] Mary was filled with the realization of one thing only, yet it was the most important thing of all, namely, that what the Archangel Gabriel was saying was true and worth committing one's entire existence to.

Mary truly believed that nothing was impossible with God.

---

[133] Luke 1:34.

[134] Luke 1:35.

[135] Luke 1:36.

[136] Luke 1:37.

[137] Luke 1:45.

[138] Luke 1:46, 48.

Her intimate collaboration in the process of our Redemption was based upon nothing other than that belief.

9. *Raphael: The Name Means "God Heals"*

The third Archangel of whom the Bible speaks by name is to be found in the Book of Tobit, a book belonging to the genre of wisdom literature, a type of literature in which teachings are imparted not as abstract precepts but rather through a story with a genuine plot that is moving, lively and interesting.

In this veritable jewel of Old Testament literature, the real protagonist is actually the Archangel Raphael, "one of the seven angels," as he describes himself, "who enter and serve the glory of the Lord." [139]

In his commentary on this sacred book, Marocco has aptly noted: "In the economy of this work, Raphael performs an essential function and the book would not be understandable without his presence. The Book of Tobit provides an important step forward in the development of doctrine on the angels."[140]

The name "Raphael" means "God heals"; it contrasts with the name of the demon Asmodeus, "the Destroyer," who also appears in the Book of Tobit.

Against this demon representing darkness and death, Raphael acts with the strength which came from God and causes the correct and spiritual understanding of marriage as part of the plan of God to provide for the mutual love of spouses and the procreation of children to triumph.

The book was narrated by Tobit, a man of integrity of spirit and generosity of heart; he was married to Anna, like himself a good and God-fearing person.

---

[139] Tobit 12:15.

[140] G. Marocco, in *La Bibbia: Parola di Dio scritta per noi* ["The Bible: Word of God Written for Us"], I, Marietti, Turin, 1980, p. 1183, note.

It is well-known that the good do not often reap the rewards of their good works during their earthly pilgrimage. That was certainly the case in the life of Tobit. During the time he spent in exile in Nineveh, for example, and notwithstanding the fact that he distinguished himself by every type of justice and good works, and particularly by the compassion he exhibited in burying the dead, Tobit nevertheless was struck blind.

His own wife, provoked by her own unhappiness, hurled this reproach of the tempter in his face: "Where now are your acts of charity; where are your righteous deeds?"[141]

Tobit was overcome with anguish. Nevertheless he turned to God with a prayer which amounted to a kind of existential cry.

With a synchronism which turns out to be quite effective in the narrative, the sorrowful prayer of Tobit at Nineveh was paralleled by the prayer of Sarah, a young woman in another country who had been married seven times, but whose successive husbands had each time been killed on the wedding night by the demon Asmodeus.

The character of Sarah in the story is intended to express the difficulties inherent in matrimony, particularly as regards the use of sex. Sex is something good in itself, but nonetheless all too capable of also playing a destructive role owing to the wound of original sin in us combined with the malevolent influence of the Devil (represented in the story by Asmodeus), thus reducing the relationship of a couple to a solely material plane.

And so it was that the Archangel Raphael was sent from God, to heal the blindness of Tobit and to remedy the painful situation of Sarah.

We encounter Raphael following the oral testament of Tobit given to his son Tobias; the latter was exhorted to live

---

141 Tobit 2:14.

according to God's law in all respects, in harmony with the precepts of justice and fraternal love, precepts which today have particular contemporary relevance.

Almost as a direct response from God to the need of such an exemplary father, Raphael appeared as a young Israelite who became the companion of Tobias, the son of Tobit, on a journey into Media on which he was sent by his father in order to collect a sum of money owed to them.

The way Tobit and Raphael became acquainted is not without interest. Tobit wanted to know the companion with whom his son would be traveling, and it was thus that Raphael was introduced into the house of Tobit. The Archangel greeted the old man with a pleasant word: "May you have much joy!" Tobit could only reply: "What joy can I have? I am blind. I live like the dead: I hear the voices of men but I cannot see them." Raphael replied with words of liberating comfort: "Be brave. God will not fail to heal you. Have courage."[142]

The old father, reassured by his conversation with his son's companion for the journey, promised to give him a monetary recompense for leading the way and providing good company.

The Archangel, appearing to be a young Jew of a good family which enjoyed an excellent reputation, reassuringly told Tobit that they would make the journey without incident and return unharmed for *the way was safe!*[143]

In fact, no journey could be safer from misfortune than one taken in the company of an angel!

Perhaps, though, this is a certitude which we who live at such a distance from the events of Scripture have yet to learn properly.

The remainder of the Book of Tobit consists of a very happy

---

[142] Cf. Tobit 5:10.

[143] Cf. Tobit 5:16.

working out of the initiatives set in motion by Raphael; the whole narrative demonstrates an angel's power to provide help.

Using a fish taken from the Tigris river, the Archangel showed Tobias how parts of this fish could be used in a medicinal way both to cure Tobit's blindness and to help remedy Sarah's persistent problem.

As regards Sarah, Raphael told Tobias plainly that she was destined to be his wife for she belonged to the same family stock he did, and his father wished him to marry within this same family line.

When Tobias nevertheless expressed his great fears, after having been informed of the deaths of her previous husbands, Raphael reassured him and advised him how to insure that the demon Asmodeus would be put to flight.

Much more touching and significant in the Book of Tobit with respect to the spirituality of matrimony, even today, is the exhortation of Raphael on the wedding night: "When you are about to go to bed with her, both of you must first stand up and pray, imploring the Lord of heaven that mercy and safekeeping may be granted to you. Do not be afraid, for she was set apart for you before the world was made. You will save her and she will go with you, and I suppose that you will have children by her."[144]

This is, in outline, an anticipation of the Christian view of marriage: in Christian marriage the spouses mutually help save one another in the sense that each one helps the other walk as "a child of the light" in Christ Jesus the Lord. Each one is God's gift to the other from all eternity. However, the gift of mutual love is truly revealed for what it is only in the light of prayer. In fact, without a strong and continuing relationship with the Lord, mutual love proves to be fragile and the couple can all too easily break up.

---

[144] Tobit 6:18.

From being one in communion with one another a couple can become isolates in desperation at the mercy of any demon like Asmodeus, who can transform the licit pleasure of sex into lust and incommunicability.

10. The Angel as Teacher

After the wedding, Raphael accompanies the newlyweds back to Nineveh and then cures Tobit of his blindness. Tobias summed up the story in this way: "He has led me back to you safely, he cured my wife, he obtained the money for you, and he also healed you."[145] "Therefore," Tobias wondered, "what ought the recompense for the companion of my journey be?"

Tobit decided that half the money the two of them had been able to bring back constituted an adequate expression of gratitude for all that had been done. It was at this point, however, that the Archangel Raphael revealed his true identity.

The discourse by which he revealed his identity is such a pearl in the fabric of the story that it is worth quoting almost in its entirety:

"Praise God and give thanks to him; exalt him and give thanks to him in the presence of all the living for what he has done for you. It is good to praise God and exalt his name, worthily declaring the works of God. Do not be slow to give him thanks... Prayer when accompanied by fasting is good, but better than either is almsgiving accompanied by righteousness. A little with righteousness is better than much with wrongdoing. It is better to give alms than to store up gold; for almsgiving saves one from death, and it will purge away every sin... I will not conceal anything from you... When you and your daughter-in-law Sarah prayed, I presented and read the record of your

[145] Tobit 12:3.

prayer before the glory of the Lord; and when you buried the dead, I did the same. When you did not hesitate to rise and leave your dinner in order to go and bury the dead, I was sent to put you to the test. At the same time, however, God sent me to heal you and your daughter-in-law Sarah. I am Raphael, one of the seven angels who enter and serve before the glory of the Lord."[146]

At this point the text focuses upon the fear of Tobit and his son. This kind of reaction of fear is recurrent when human beings become aware that they have actually entered into contact with persons from the world beyond.

The final words of parting in this text are quite valuable: Raphael "said to them, 'Do not be afraid; you will be safe. But praise God forever. For I did not come as a favor on my part, but by the will of our God. Therefore praise him forever.'"

Speaking very clearly, he added a few words about his own mode of being: "Even though you watched me eat and drink, I did not really do so; what you were seeing was a vision. So now give thanks to God, for I am about to ascend to him who sent me. Write down everything that has happened."[147]

From everything which the Book of Tobit tells us about the Archangel Raphael, some definite ideas clearly emerge about the identity of the angels and about how they serve as messengers from God to man.

First of all, it is evident that angels exist to praise and thank God, and that they seek to involve us, their human brothers in a lower kingdom, in this same purely spiritual work of thanks and praise.

Then, secondly, the angels are the inspirers of those good and just actions which help man realize himself in accord with God's plan, the plan for which, before the advent of original sin, man was made in God's "image and likeness." It was always

---

[146] Tobit 12:6-16.

[147] Tobit 12:17-20.

part of this plan of God that man would participate in it. Even after original sin, this divine "image and likeness" in man can be reconstituted in those who live "the perfect law... of liberty,"[148] that is, the law of love, free of all greed, selfishness and injustice.

As for prayer, it is important to understand the role of the Archangel in the prayer offered by Tobias and Sarah.

St. Thomas Aquinas taught with good reason that the angels help us in the work of contemplation, manifesting divine realities to us, fortifying our minds, and preventing us from getting mired down in vain and harmful imaginings.[149]

Angels are sent to test the faith of men. While God permits us to be tempted by demons, the interventions of the angels are entirely beneficent, helping to remedy in us whatever is weak, fragile, and inclined to evil.

The greeting of the Archangel, then, and his discreet encouragement to do good are for the purpose of promoting serenity and peace.

His words, "Do not be afraid; you will be safe," represent a typical kind of greeting and reassurance that would become characteristic of the Gospels.

And when, with the Resurrection, the redemptive work of Jesus was completed, it was precisely with such words as these that Jesus greeted those to whom he appeared.

In any case, as has been said, Jesus is the Angel of the Father par excellence, the one sent by the Father who truly is able to save.

The concluding teachings of Raphael, which still enlighten us about the reality of angels, certainly confirm the fact of their incorporeal nature. More than that, though, they bear out that the angels do not come to us and remain with us out of any

---

[148] James 1:25.

[149] Cf. St. Thomas Aquinas, *Summa Theologica*, I q. 111, a. 4; I-II, q. 9, a. 6; II-II, q. 122, a. 2.

personal initiative or wish of their own. Rather, they come because such is the will of God.

There is one final observation to be made regarding the long "poem" delivered by Raphael.

The young Tobias departed on his long journey at the behest of his father accompanied, to be sure, by an angel but also accompanied by his dog. "So they both went out and departed, and the young man's dog was with them."[150]

This is a telling detail which enables us to read, in its cosmic dimension, not only the narrative itself, but indeed the whole of human existence.

Immersed in an amazing world of absolute marvels, we are nevertheless "subject to frailty" as we journey towards our true home.

We enjoy the angels as escorts although we do not see them.

We also have the animals on our journey with us; them we do see.

And over them we sometimes exercise a haughty kind of dominion which is often violent and ungrateful; occasionally we use them as objects, in the manner of playthings for our pleasure.

Instead, the proper way to relate to them ought to be with joy and gratitude and praise to God!

Once we have learned to look upon them thus benevolently as gifts of God provided for our service, we should be similarly prompted to look upwards to those other spiritual creatures who are likewise gifts to us from the same Creator and who are even greater friends to us!

In the end it is an affair of the heart: through what we are able to see we should become habituated to trying to take in all of reality, even that which may be invisible to the physical eye.

[150] Tobit 6:2.

3

ANGELS IN THE LIFE OF CHRIST

1. *Angels and the Birth and Infancy of Christ*

To believe means to look at history as a single salvific event.

Towards Christ, the heart and center of humanity, flow rivers of shadow and light, the ages which came before and will come after him. The existence of each one of us draws its significance from the fact that Christ became incarnate, lived as a man, was put to death, and then rose again from the dead for the salvation of all, from the most gifted to the most limited, from the most intelligent to the most mentally handicapped, from primitive cave-dwellers to those who will live in an even more highly sophisticated technological society tomorrow.

Precisely "when the fulness of time had come,"[151] and the infinite Word (Wisdom) of the Father had become man, the angels had their work cut out for them as the messengers of God in the service of Christ who was himself "the Angel (Messenger) of the Father" for purposes of our salvation, as well as the "Head of the Angels," according to the papal encyclical *Mystici Corporis*.

Even though Jesus assumed a human nature, a nature inferior to that of the angels, being the very Person of the Word,

[151] Galatians 4:4.

"God from God, light from light,"[152] he was infinitely superior to the angels even while he was here on earth.

It is both fitting and meaningful to focus at this point on the angels in the life of Christ. At certain significant moments their presence was visible but he was certainly never without their invisible presence around him for the entire period of his sojourn on earth.

As we have already seen, it was the Archangel Gabriel who was the herald sent to announce to Mary the ineffable mystery of the plan God had in mind.

At the time of the birth of Jesus, the angels were especially active. The pages of the Gospel according to Luke specifically reflect the joy of this fact.

Near the little town of Bethlehem, where Jesus first saw the light of day, "there were shepherds out in the field, keeping watch over their flock by night. And an angel of the Lord appeared to them, and the glory of the Lord shone around them, and they were filled with fear. Then an angel said to them, 'Be not afraid; for behold, I bring you good news of a great joy which will come to all the people; for to you is born this day in the city of David a Savior, who is Christ the Lord. And this will be a sign for you: you will find a babe wrapped in swaddling cloths and lying in a manger.' And suddenly there was with the angel a multitude of the heavenly host praising God and saying, 'Glory to God in the highest, and on earth peace among men with whom he is pleased!'"[153]

The angel who thus communicated the good news of the birth of Jesus to the shepherds was truly a messenger of joy; all the other angels who praised God under the skies of Bethlehem were similarly messengers of peace.

"Do not be afraid," the Archangel Gabriel had told Mary

[152] Cf. Hebrews 1:4 ff.; 2:7-9.

[153] Luke 2:8-14.

when she was troubled at such an unusual approach and greeting on his part.

"Be not afraid," the angel also declared to the shepherds, who were likewise understandably frightened. But the Kingdom of God is "righteousness and peace and joy in the Holy Spirit."[154] In Jesus we did not "receive the spirit of slavery to fall back into fear but... the spirit of sonship."[155]

Thus the angels are, so to speak, the heralds, communicators, cheer-leaders and co-workers in this new "Kingdom" which finally, with the coming of Jesus, had found a place in the world of men.

Moreover, even today, each time someone commits himself to Christ and to the hierarchy of values which follow from that commitment, the same "be not afraid" of the angels is repeated for him. Indeed it is *the most authentic proclamation of peace and joy imaginable.* It penetrates the being of anyone who commits himself to Christ and makes room for the Kingdom. Invisibly and notwithstanding the darkness, the difficulty and the pain in an individual's heart and life, the angels of the Lord convince him of what the Kingdom of God is all about.

From this comes the efficacy of the Christian witness, that visible aspect of hope which shines in the face and in the actions of those who have become Christ's apostles.

With regard to the angels who were present at the birth of Christ, I believe it is encouraging to recall a double affirmation about them made by the Fathers of the Church and repeated by Jean Daniélou.

"The angelic mystery of the Nativity consists above all in the presence of the angels assigned to every nation surrounding the infant God who had come to aid the various pagan peoples

---

[154] Romans 14:17.

[155] Romans 8:15.

entrusted to them and for whose sake they were accustomed to spend themselves so tirelessly."[156]

The angels in charge of regulating the entire cosmos, as Daniélou likewise affirmed following the lead of the Fathers of the Church, also recognized in Jesus the King of the universe and, while continuing their usual mission of bringing all things back to God, at the same time, they freely and spontaneously subjected themselves to Christ the Lord whom they recognized to be so much more powerful than all of them.

It was through the ministry of an angel that Joseph, troubled by the signs of Mary's maternity, of whose origin he was not aware, was reassured.

And it was this same silent "just man" who was led by angels at the time of the flight into Egypt, and later to return again to Judea.

Angels assigned to various nations and peoples as well as those in charge of regulating various aspects of the cosmos are all drawn to Christ.

Perhaps the most daring position taken by any of the Fathers of the Church on the angels and their relationship to the coming of Christ was the one taken by Origen, who expressed himself thus on the subject: "When the angels saw the Prince of the heavenly host come down to earth to dwell, they too took the route which the Lord had opened up, acting in obedience to him, the Master who assigned them their various tasks of watching over those who believed in him. Thus, the angels are in the service of your salvation. They were assigned to the Son of God to follow him. And among themselves they would say: 'If he has come down into a body what excuse do we have for remaining idle? Let us all descend from heaven too.' It was thus that a great multitude of the heavenly host was to be found praising and glorifying God at the moment of his birth in Bethlehem. *The world is filled with Angels!*"[157]

[156] J. Daniélou, op. cit., pp. 35-46.

[157] Origen, *Hom. in Ez.*, 1, 7.

2. *Angels at the Service of Christ*

If the birth and infancy of Christ were accompanied by the visible presence of the angels, the same thing was true of other important periods in his life among us: the angels were present at those times too.

Immediately prior to the beginning of his public life, "Jesus was led by the Spirit into the wilderness to be tempted by the Devil."[158]

In one of the three great temptations presented to him by the Devil, the latter, with persuasive words, suggested that Jesus should throw himself down from the pinnacle of the Temple in Jerusalem, since, as was recorded in Scripture (Psalm 91), "He will give his angels charge of you; on their hands, they will bear you up, lest you strike your foot against a stone."

This sacrilegious use of a quotation from the Psalms by the tempter included, interestingly enough, a sarcastic allusion by the demon to those spiritual beings who were like himself in all things except that they had remained faithful to God.

Jesus naturally rejected this temptation from the Devil by quoting Scripture himself: "You shall not put the Lord your God to the test."[159]

Following the last temptation, which involved abandoning fidelity to God for the sake of worldly power, Jesus explicitly rejected and repudiated Satan by quoting yet another scriptural passage: "You shall fear the Lord your God; you shall serve him, and swear by his name."[160] For Jesus, the most efficacious of all weapons in spiritual warfare was nothing other than the Word of God.

At this point the evangelist Matthew notes: "Then the Devil left him, and, behold, angels came and ministered to him."[161]

---

[158] Matthew 4:1.

[159] Deuteronomy 6:16.

[160] Deuteronomy 6:13.

[161] Matthew 4:11.

That which Jesus had refused to ask for as a miracle which would in no way have redounded to the glory of his Father — was given to him as a free gift anyhow: the ministry of the angels in his service.

The Son of God chose to remain faithful in every detail to the plan of his Father — and thus he remained wholly free from desiring the illusory goals put forward by the Devil.

It was for this reason that his Father sent the angels to minister to him.

This same lesson applies to our lives also, at least to the lives of those of us who realize that the moral choices we make in life have consequences. The Devil seeks to hem us in by tempting us at crucial moments with the facile illusions of hedonism, vainglory, and worldly power.

If, however, we remain faithful in our recourse to God, we ward off the assaults of the Devil, and, for a time at least, he is constrained to leave us alone.

The angels crowd around to help us; they fill our lives with peace and holy inspiration.

Another extremely important moment in the life of Christ, of course, was his agony in the Garden of Gethsemane. When his acute anguish over the sin of the world touched the very depths of his being, Jesus emitted a very human cry to God. At the same time it was a cry worthy of the Holy One of God, the One in whom the Father was well-pleased: "Father, if you are willing, take this cup from me; still not my will, but yours, be done." "Then," the evangelist Luke goes on to add, "there appeared to him an angel from heaven, strengthening him."[162]

At the culminating moment of his life when, through his human nature, the person of Christ was facing death itself, an angel — a being inferior to him who was God, but stronger than him who suffered entirely as a man — was sent by the Father to comfort him in response to his heartfelt cry.

---

[162] Luke 22:42-43.

The angel brought reassurance; he did not eliminate the suffering itself. Indeed Luke wrote how immediately afterwards "[Christ's] sweat became like great drops of blood falling down upon the ground."[163] The same thing often occurs when we pray during times of great difficulty. God loves us too much simply to eliminate hardships from our lives miraculously. He does, however, comfort us by means of the angels who stimulate in us new courage with which to confront our old difficulties.

Neither the granting of prayers nor the comfort which comes to us from God are intended to substitute for the free will we have been given with which to chart the course of our faith on the path to salvation, a path which necessarily leads through some rough and difficult terrain.

It is appropriate to mention here another reflection touching upon the relationship of Jesus with the angels.

The angels are in his service. He could have made particular use of them at any and every moment of his earthly existence (over which he enjoyed absolute sovereignty).

Yet he made use of the services of the angels only insofar as this accorded with his Father's plan.

As we saw, he rejected the proposals of Satan out of hand. He did, however, consent to be ministered to by the angels after the period of his temptations had been completed, just as he consented to be comforted by an angel in his agony; but he also willingly, knowingly, and freely willed to be delivered into the hands of his oppressors without calling for help, and this solely because "his hour had come."

"Put your sword back in its place," he said to one of his followers who had attempted to defend him with a sword when his enemies arrived to arrest him. "Do you think," he demanded, "that I cannot appeal to my Father, and he will at once send me more than twelve legions of angels? But how then should the Scriptures be fulfilled that it must be so?"[164]

---

[163] Luke 22:44.

[164] Matthew 26:52-54.

With respect to these particular words, it appears evident that Jesus' irrefutable awareness of being the Son of God included an awareness that he had veritable legions of angels prepared to serve him. Yet this very affirmation of Christ underlines the fact of his free choice to empty himself totally, even to the point of being delivered, defenceless, into the very jaws of death, death on a cross.

For, as Jesus himself foretold, once the Redemption had been accomplished, the angels themselves were going to be the ones to sing the splendid victory of it all: "You will see the heavens opened, and the angels of God ascending and descending upon the Son of Man."[165]

It was not by accident that the Book of Revelation depicts the magnificent drama of the Lamb that was slain as a great eschatological transfiguration and celebration of joy. And among the voices celebrating, of course, were the voices of many angels: "'Worthy is the Lamb who was slain, to receive power and wealth and wisdom and might and honor and glory and blessing.' And I heard every creature in heaven and on earth and under the earth and in the sea, and all therein saying, 'To him who sits upon the throne and to the Lamb be blessing and honor and glory and might for ever and ever!'"[166]

With respect to the mysterious influence which the passion of Christ had upon the angels and on their relationship with men, it is worth quoting a reflection made by St. Augustine: "Christ did not die for the angels. Nevertheless everything that was accomplished through the Redemption effected by Christ was to the advantage of the angels because, with the Redemption of man, the damage which had originated with the ruin of the angels was repaired. It is certain that the holy angels, who know God directly and are blessed in this direct contemplation of truth, also know how many members of the human race they

[165] John 1:51.

[166] Revelation 5:11-13.

await in order that the number of citizens of the holy city might be reconstituted."[167]

This reflection of St. Augustine appears to underscore a very fruitful line of thought, one which recalls St. Paul's words to the effect that Christ unites or sums up "all things in him[self], things in heaven and things on earth."[168] This reflection should rekindle in us another reason for the call that has been made to us to share in a life of fulfillment, joy, and infinite harmony in heaven. For the fact is that we are awaited in heaven precisely in order that we may fill those places left empty there by the rebellious angels.

Through Christ, in Christ, and with Christ we will one day sound the notes currently lacking in the symphony being played by our companions of light.

3. *Angels and the Risen Christ*

It is interesting to reconstruct from the accounts of the synoptic Gospels the way in which the angels functioned at that very central moment in the life of Christ which marked the defeat of sin and death, namely, the Resurrection.

Matthew noted that *"an angel of the Lord descended from heaven* and came and rolled back the stone, and sat upon it. And behold... his appearance was like lightning, and his raiment white as snow. And for fear of him the guards trembled and became like dead men."[170]

Meanwhile a cosmic earthquake accompanied all this and, in a certain sense, marked the key event in the history of salvation.

[167] St. Augustine, in *La Teologia dei Padri* ["The Theology of the Fathers"], Citta Nuova, Rome, 1975, p. 11.

[168] Ephesians 1:10.

[169] Cf. St. Thomas Aquinas, *Summa Theologica*, I, q. 9, a. 63.

[170] Matthew 28:2-4.

Mark, with his usual incisiveness, also spoke about the angel, presenting him through the eyes of Mary Magdalene, Mary, the mother of James, and Salome: "Entering the tomb, *they saw a young man* sitting on the right side, dressed in a white robe; *and they were amazed*."[171]

According to Luke, *two* angels appeared, and, as is often the case in other biblical texts, these angels were called "men." The context, however, gives us to understand that only the appearance of a man was what was really involved; behind this appearance there were real supernatural beings present: the women "found the stone rolled away from the tomb, but when they went in they did not find the body. While they were perplexed about this, behold, *two men stood by them in dazzling apparel, and as they were frightened [they] bowed their faces to the ground....*"[172]

The elements that are common to these accounts of angelic appearances are quite important: the dazzling aspect, the youthful freshness and vitality but also and above all, the unusual character of an encounter with the supernatural invariably inspiring the emotion of fear.

More important yet, however, was the *kind of message* delivered by the angels in this most consequential of salvific moments.

In Matthew's account the angel said to the women: "Do not be afraid; for I know that you seek Jesus who was crucified. He is not here; for he has risen, as he said. Come, see the place where he lay. Then go quickly and tell his disciples that he has risen from the dead, and behold he is going before you to Galilee; there you will see him. Lo, I have told you."[173]

Mark's account, as usual, is more concise,[174] but it basically

[171] Mark 16:5.

[172] Luke 24:1-5.

[173] Matthew 28:5-7.

[174] Cf. Mark 16:4-7.

emphasizes the same essential points about what has occurred: there is the invitation not to be afraid, the announcement of the Resurrection of Christ, and an exhortation to communicate this unique fact to the disciples "and Peter" (Mark, the spokesman for the memories and teachings of Peter on whom Jesus founded his Church, adds this significant detail).

In Luke, the angelic message is more clearly articulated and its significance thereby brought out. It was not by accident that the evangelist who noted with such care the presence of the angels at the birth of Jesus should be the same evangelist most attentive to the message of the angels at the point where Christ achieved the summit of his earthly existence with his Resurrection from the dead.

According to Luke, the angel said to the women who had come to the tomb: "Why do you seek the living among the dead? He is not here, but has risen. Remember how he told you while he was still in Galilee, that the Son of Man must be delivered into the hands of sinful men, and be crucified, and on the third day rise."[175]

This message brought into sharp relief the identity of Christ as the angels saw him; according to them, Christ was *the "One Who Lives,"* the living person par excellence. To seek for him among the dead or among those ignorant of where to find the fullness of life would be to seek him in vain.

More important still is the fact that the angels referred to Christ's own prophecies as a proof of the authenticity of the Resurrection.[176]

In the final analysis, the angels were always referring back to Scripture, as Jesus himself did, when he explained the Scriptures to the two disciples on the road to Emmaus.[177]

There is, therefore, an intimate relationship between the

---

175 Luke 24:5-7.

176 Luke 9:22.

177 Cf. Luke 24:13-32.

presence of the angels, their mission in the history of salvation, and Scripture, the Word of God itself, ignorance of which, according to St. Jerome, is ignorance of Christ.[178]

It is in view of all this that we can understand how an enlightened devotion to the angels, far from distracting us from Christ or getting us off on the wrong devotional track, will actually lead us deeper into the mystery of Christ who is to be adored, and will help us "take refuge in the Gospel as we do in the flesh of Jesus Christ himself."[179]

4. *Angels and the Mystery of the Ascension of Jesus into Heaven*

In the Acts of the Apostles, Luke indicates a presence of angels with the same kind of narrative style he employed in his Gospel with respect to the Resurrection.

The final words of the earthly message of Jesus were recorded in Acts: "You shall receive power when the Holy Spirit has come upon you; and you shall be my witnesses in Jerusalem and in Judea and Samaria and to the end of the earth."

Having said this, Jesus was raised up before their eyes and disappeared from their sight behind a cloud. While they were gazing up after him "*two men stood by them in white robes* and said: 'Men of Galilee, why do you stand looking into heaven? This Jesus, who was taken up from you into heaven, will come in the same way as you saw him go into heaven.'"[180]

It is very significant that, in this "epilogue" of the story of Christ on earth, there should have been a presence of angels and, moreover, that they should have prophesied concerning Christ's ultimate return in glory.[181]

---

[178] Cf. St. Jerome, *Comm. in Is.* 1, 2.

[179] St. Ignatius of Antioch, *To the Philadelphians* 5:1.

[180] Acts 1:8-11.

[181] Cf. John 1:51.

The Fathers of the Church insisted on the presence of the angels at the Ascension; this was true to such a point that they liked to describe these angels as providing a triumphal escort for Jesus, while accompanying him into the glory of heaven, singing loud hosannas all the while.

Eusebius of Caesarea, for example, wrote in this vein: "The celestial Virtues, seeing him ascending, circled around him to provide an escort, proclaiming this Ascension of his with the words: 'Lift up your heads, O gates! and be lifted up, O ancient doors! that the King of glory may come in!'[182] This was fulfilled in the Ascension of Christ as recorded in the Acts of the Apostles."[183]

This Christological reading of the Psalms in connection with the Ascension allowed the Fathers of the Church to emphasize the presence of the angels. This way of thinking has found an even more profound application today in the work of a writer such as Jean Daniélou, who wrote on the subject: "The relationship of the angels with the Ascension is an integral part of the mystery itself. It is more than just a question of the elevation of Christ's body in the midst of the angels. Theologically speaking, *it is the exaltation of the human nature assumed by the Word of God above the level of the angelic orders naturally superior to this human nature.* This transformation of the normal situation represented a truly unexpected turn of events for the angels."[184]

St. Paul, writing to the Ephesians, said that God had manifested "his great might which he accomplished in Christ when he raised him from the dead and made him sit at his right hand in the heavenly places, far above all rule and authority and power and dominion, and above every name that is named... and he has put all things under his feet."[185]

---

[182] Psalm 24:9.

[183] Eusebius of Caesarea, *Comm. In Ps. 17.*

[184] J. Daniélou, op. cit., p. 49.

[185] Ephesians 1:19-22.

When we take in and grasp the fullness and diversity of the entire angelic panorama, we take in and grasp more perfectly the mystery of Christ himself,[186] the fact that he sums up everything in creation, reflects the glory of God, and bears the stamp of his own divine nature: "When he had made purification for sins, he sat down at the right hand of the Majesty on high, having become as much superior to angels as the name he has obtained is more excellent than theirs."[187]

It is worthwhile quoting Jean Daniélou again on this subject; according to him, "the mystery of the Ascension threw the angels in heaven into a state of great surprise. What was revealed by the Ascension was truly a mystery which had been hidden up until then, an absolutely new reality... The real mystery behind the Nativity was the abasement of the divine Person of the Word to a state a little 'lower than the angels.'[188] The true mystery of the Ascension lay in the exaltation of human nature to a state above that of the angels."[189]

Precisely because the good angels remained free of the blurred vision brought on by sin, they have been able to penetrate more freely and more deeply into this ineffable mystery; for this reason, they can help us, even today, to draw closer to the living Christ with our own nature glorified by him, and thus to love him with the thrust of our whole being.

St. Gregory of Nyssa wrote quite aptly about the power of the angels "to penetrate the multiple aspects of a wisdom conscious of fundamental contrasts such as seeing the Word made flesh, death in the midst of life, our wounds healed by the stripes of his martyrdom, the strength of our adversary vanquished by the weakness of the cross, and the invisible manifested in the flesh."[190]

---

[186] Cf. Ephesians 1:9.

[187] Hebrews 1:3-4.

[188] Hebrews 2:7.

[189] Jean Daniélou, op. cit., p. 55.

[190] St. Gregory of Nyssa, *Hom. in Cant.* 8.

To the jealousy manifested by the rebellious angels, who were unwilling to accept the marvelous plan of God to restore a fallen humanity, there was the benevolence of the faithful angels towards "the new man."

The fact is that man was wonderfully restored in Christ through a dynamism which, according to St. Ephraem, unites man "to the Principalities, Powers, Thrones, and Dominations *in a common celebration*."[191]

In the end, to invoke the angels means above all to obtain a dynamism by which the faith, hope, and charity already present in us from baptism will become living and active in our everyday lives.

From being merely baptized persons, it is imperative that we go on to become followers of Christ in a real way; for that reason we are called to walk here below in the happy anticipation of an eternal marriage in heaven: that in which our companions of the light, the angels, are already immersed.

[191] St. Ephraem, *Serm. Nat.*, PG 44, 1129B.

4

ANGELS IN THE LIFE OF THE CHURCH

1. *Angels and the Initial Building Up of the Church*

There can be no doubt that our sense of the mystery of the Church becomes deepened when it is contemplated in the light of the centrality of Christ the Lord. This kind of contemplation should not neglect, however, to include also the presence of the angels and what they have brought to the life of the Church. The Fathers of the Church greatly emphasized the theme of the angels as collaborators of Christ in the founding and building up of the Church.

We only need to recall in this regard the ancient Christian document known as *The Shepherd of Hermas*. In this work we read: "The tower I see is the Church. It is built on water because our life found its salvation in water.[192] The six youths are the holy angels, created first by God. God confided to them the care of all creatures, that they might help them prosper by organizing and governing them; it was through them that the Church was to be built up."[193]

In the Acts of the Apostles we read that the angels purposely vied with one another in helping to build up the primi-

[192] This is a clear reference to Baptism.

[193] Hermas, *Il Pastore* ["The Shepherd"], Vision III, 3, 3-4; Cf. also ibid., *Similitudine*, IX, 12, 78.

tive Church; they freed the apostles from prison, opening wide the prison doors for them, and giving them very clear and precise indications of what, with all candor and courage, they were to do: "Go and stand in the Temple and speak to the people all *these words of life*."[194]

And to Peter, in particular — symbol, foundation, and head of the Church —another angel offered assistance which, in the description which the Acts provides, is quite significant precisely with respect to the intervention of the angels in helping to build up the Church.

Not only did the angel free Peter from his chains and lead him out of the prison, but he even went before him into the streets of the city. At first Peter believed that he was doing all this in a dream or vision. Coming to himself, however, Peter said: "Now I am sure that the Lord has sent his angel and rescued me from the hands of Herod and from all that the Jewish people were expecting."[195]

The Acts of the Apostles, of course, focuses on a number of other extraordinary interventions by the angels in these very early days of the Church.

Cornelius was not a Jew, but a pagan, "a centurion of what was known as the Italian cohort."[196] He saw an "angel standing in his house and saying, 'Send to Joppa and bring Simon who is called Peter; he will declare to you a message by which you will be saved, you and all your household.'"[197]

It was not by accident that the first pagan officially admitted into the Church community was guided to the Church by an angel. The approach of this angel was like a beacon of hope and confidence for him. The celestial messenger said to him, in fact:

[194] Acts 5:20.

[195] Acts 12:11.

[196] Acts 10:1.

[197] Acts 11:13-14.

"Your prayers and your alms have ascended as a memorial before God."[198]

The Ethiopian eunuch, "a court official of the Candace, Queen of the Ethiopians, in charge of her whole treasury," only happened to meet Philip (one of the seven deacons appointed by the apostles in Jerusalem to serve the Church) through a special angelic intervention. In this case, the celestial messenger had expressly said to the new deacon: "Rise and go toward the south to the road that goes down from Jerusalem to Gaza."[199]

This man of the Lord obeyed the angel's instructions, and it was thus that he was given an opportunity to explain the prophecy of Isaiah to the Ethiopian who was reading it but unable to understand its meaning. The meeting not only resulted in an evangelization but ended in an immediate total surrender to Christ which is often experienced by those who are thunderstruck by the power of the Word of God: "The eunuch said: 'See, here is water! What is to prevent my being baptized?' And he commanded the chariot to stop, and they both went down into the water, Philip and the eunuch, and [Philip] baptized him. When they came up out of the water... the eunuch went on his way rejoicing."[200]

At the origin of Philip's pastoral ministry to the eunuch, then, there was a suggestion, an inspiration, on the part of an angel. The fruits reaped were clearly enumerated in the sacred text: the conversion of a pagan, access to the life of Christ and the Church by means of baptism, and the joy of the Spirit which fills those who are vivified by the Spirit.

Paul, the Apostle of the Gentiles, having appealed his case to Caesar, since he had been unjustly accused, embarked for Italy. A tremendous storm arose battering the ship and crew

---

[198] Acts 10:4.

[199] Acts 8:26.

[200] Acts 8:36-39.

until they were at the end of their strength and on the point of despair.

Paul, however, spoke in this vein to these men of the sea: "I urge you now to take heart; for there will be no loss of life among you, but only of the ship. For last night there stood by me an angel of the God to whom I belong and whom I worship, and he said, 'Do not be afraid, Paul. You must stand before Caesar; and so God has granted safety to you and to all those who are sailing with you.' Therefore, take heart, men. I have faith in God that it will be exactly as I have been told."[201]

Even though the scriptural accounts of all these supernatural interventions do not have "to be taken literally in all their details,"[202] it would be foolish to exclude the fact that the angels played a special role in the initial establishment of the Church within a universalism that would involve every race and nation.

2. *Angels and the Mystery of the Church*

"The immortal and blessed spirits who are deservedly established in heavenly abodes and rejoice in communion with their Creator are rooted in his eternity, certain in his truth, and sanctified in his grace. In their compassion they love us unhappy mortals and long for us to become both immortal and happy. And, therefore, they do not wish us to offer sacrifice to them but to God, knowing as they do that, along with us, they are his sacrifice. For *we, together with them, form one City of God* to which the psalmist addressed the words: 'Glorious things are said of you, O city of God.'[203] *Of this city our part is still on pilgrimage, while the other part, the angels, help to guide us.*"[204]

---

[201] Acts 27:22-26.

[202] Cf. A.M. Canopi, op. cit., 14, 10.

[203] Psalm 87:3.

[204] St. Augustine, *The City of God*, 10, 7.

Here, with his accustomed vigor, St. Augustine has presented the Church to us as "the City of God," of which the angels form a part, having been charged by God with assisting us, "the pilgrim Church" here on earth. In yet another text, this towering genius of Christianity presents the same broad horizons when he speaks of the mystery of the Church which includes the angels: "The temple of God, that is, the temple of the sublime Trinity, is the holy Church herself in her fullness, both in heaven and on earth... That part of the Church between the holy angels and the powers of God will be manifest when we are finally united with her in the possession of everlasting beatitude."[205]

Considering the clarity and limpidity of his doctrine, how can we fail to quote St. Augustine again at this point?

"The City of God must be considered in its totality, and not only that part of it which continues to undergo its pilgrimage on earth. This part must give continual praise to the name of the Lord from dawn until dusk. Delivered from its slavery, it must continue to sing a new song,[206] joining with the other part of the City of God which remains in heaven with its Creator... This second part of the Church is found among the holy angels in eternal beatitude, and, as is just and fitting, descends to earth in order to provide aid for the pilgrim Church here below. These two parts of the City of God [the Church Militant and the Church Triumphant] will one day constitute a single City of God in the enjoyment of eternity, just as both parts are already one in the bond of charity."[207]

St. Mesrop the Armenian (5th century) stressed the sublime dignity of man called by God to exercise a "royal dominion" over the whole creation, even though as a "tester" and "praiser" of the works of the Creator. To pass "from corruption

[205] St. Augustine, in *La Teologia dei Padri* ["The Theology of the Fathers"], op. cit., IV, Rome, 1975, p. 17.

[206] Cf. Revelation 14:3.

[207] St. Augustine, *The City of God*, 12, 4.

to a state of goodness, from slavery to the liberty of the children of God, growing in the true faith in the Father, Son, and Holy Spirit in order to become inheritors of the Kingdom as well as of eternal beatitude" all this is precisely what the sons and daughters of the Church have been called to do.

It is of interest to our theme what this author said about the Creator of everything who made these spirits for his service, and the heavenly host for flames of fire. As for human beings, this author added: "Those who received the good news from the angels, are formed by the angels in the spiritual life in accordance with divine Providence which provides the Law as needed."[208]

With impressive imagery, the angels are described in the Book of Revelation as intent on offering "golden bowls full of incense, which are the prayers of the saints."[209]

With respect to our present state of being a "Pilgrim Church," which draws its strength and courage from prayer in order to realize the will of the Father, the following passage from Origen seems to me to be especially appropriate: "There is one alone to whom we must offer supplication: almighty God himself... Just as a body in motion is followed by its own shadow, so by the grace of God is the supreme God followed by the benevolence of the angels....

"They are not only supportive of human beings but help them in their desire to praise God by praying and imploring Him along with them. So true is this that we even dare to maintain that together with those who have chosen to seek the good and hence who have given themselves to prayer, there are thousands of celestial powers who pray along with them (even when they are not specifically invoked) and thus offer them help."[210]

---

[208] St. Mesrop the Armenian, "Second Discourse," in *La Teologia dei Padri*, op. cit., I, Rome, 1974, pp. 130-131.

[209] Revelation 5:8.

[210] Origen, *Contra Celsus*, 8, 64.

In a life of St. Pachomius,[211] we read that, in a vision, this saint saw the whole Church filled with angels.

As an ancient Coptic homily expressed it: "The Church is a place of consolation and a point of assembly for the angels. The Church provides the environment where the Cherubim and Seraphim congregate."[212]

St. John Damascene, in his *Exposition of the Orthodox Faith,* did not hesitate to speak of the angels and their part in the whole plan of God in which the mystery of the Church, of which we also are a part, is to be found as well: "So prompt and vigorous are they in fulfilling the will of God, so swift of movement are the angels that they always immediately find themselves exactly where the will of God has assigned them to be. Some of them watch over and regulate the various parts of the earth; they preside over nations and regions in accordance with the will and command of the supreme Creator; they govern our affairs and provide us with help... even as they remain in attendance around God himself."[213]

With regard to the missionary vocation of the Church, more than one of the ancient Fathers discerned in the angels a capability of providing effective help to those who instructed, formed, and led others to the faith.

Those angels who in Hebrew theology had been called "Angels of the Nations"[214] became, according to the New Testament, "Angels of the Church."

The Fathers of the Church who discerned this capability in the angels found and justified it from the text where John in the Book of Revelation spoke certain words concerning the seven churches of Asia Minor.[215]

---

211 *Pachomii Vita,* 104, 16.

212 Worrel, *Coptic Manuscripts (Freer Collection),* p. 356.

213 St. John Damascene, *Esposizione della fede ortodossa,* 2, 3.

214 They were called "angels of the people"; Cf. *Enoch,* LXXXIX, 59.

215 Cf. Revelation 2:3-4.

Thus, it is not out of place to quote here what St. Gregory of Nazianzen wrote on this subject apropos of his own diocese: "The care of this church has been confided to an angel. Other angels preside over other local churches, as can be deduced from the Book of Revelation."[217]

Origen had affirmed pretty much the same thing: "It can be said, following the Scriptures, that there are really two bishops over each local church, one visible and the other invisible; they are charged with carrying out the same task."[218]

It is tempting to cite some of the other available patristic texts, thus drinking deeply from the spring of ecclesiastical truth.

Let one more quotation suffice, however, this one from the authoritative St. Hippolytus of Rome (3rd century). Comparing the Church to a ship, he declared: "The Church has her special guiding pilots too, on both the port and starboard sides: I mean her attending angels. The Church has never ceased being guided and protected by the angels."[219]

As the final "draught" from the patristic spring of ecclesiastical truth, renewing in us our confidence in and esteem for the angels, let us return once more to *The Shepherd of Hermas*.

According to this source, the angel of repentance intervenes whenever it is pointed out to him that, in spite of good intentions, human beings have been caught in the snares of the devil: "I say to you," Hermas wrote, "do not fear the devil because I have been sent to be with you who, from the bottom of your heart, do penance, in order to confirm you in your faith. Have confidence in God, you who have despaired of your life

---

[216] This doctrine was common to various Fathers of the Church from Origen on; Origen interpreted the second and third chapters of the Book of Revelation in this way.

[217] St. Gregory Nazianzus, *Orat.* XLII, PG 36, 469AB.

[218] Origen, *Hom. in Luc*, 13.

[219] St. Hippolytus of Rome, *De Antichristo*, 40.

because of your sins... In fact, if you will turn to the Lord with all your heart, practice just deeds for the rest of your days, and serve God according to his will, God will heal you from your sins and give you power to triumph over the works of the devil."[220]

3. *Angels and the Dynamism of the Christian Life*

The dynamism of the Christian life is the bursting forth within us of the life of Christ which comes to us through the sacraments, making it possible for us to live out our fundamental vocation: the call to love. By means of Baptism, we are grafted onto Christ as shoots are grafted onto a vine.

By means of Confirmation we receive the strength of the Holy Spirit in such a way as to enable us to live as adults in the following of Christ.

By means of the sacrament of Reconciliation, we become reconciled to God and restored in Christ following the devastation caused in us by each and every sin.

The Eucharist reinvigorates "the new man" in us since it is "the bread of life" for our difficult pilgrimage here below.

The sacraments of Matrimony and Holy Orders make it possible for us to carry out our Christian duties in accordance with the states of life to which we are called.

Finally the sacrament of the Anointing of the Sick sustains us in the laborious task of our definitive birth: into everlasting life.

Even here, though, it is "through him, with him, and in him" that our Christian lives derive their origin, grow, and are productive even to the point of achieving that fullness and splendor which we know as sanctity.

While keeping this necessary Christocentric vision always clearly in mind, however, we should in no way overlook the role

[220] Hermas, *The Shepherd*, Precept XII, 36.

which the angels play in watching over us and in influencing us to accept Christ and the assistance of the sacraments.

The lesson of the early Church can be very useful to us in this regard.

In the early Church catechumens were invited to pray that God might "deign to send his holy angel to watch over his servants and lead them to the grace of Baptism."[221]

The ancient texts which highlight the presence of the angels in the initial sacrament of the Christian life, Baptism, are actually quite numerous.

Origen, for example, wrote: "When the sacrament of faith was given to you, the celestial virtues, the ministry of the angels, the Church of God's firstborn, were present there."[222]

St. Ambrose, in his treatise on the sacraments, focused on the wonder and joy exhibited by the angels when they realized what a marvelous thing was effected by Baptism: "The angels are caught up in admiration. Do you want to know to what point they are thus caught up in admiration? Listen to the apostle Peter, then, who speaks of 'things [announced to you] into which the angels long to look.'"[223]

If the scope of this book permitted, we could cite at some length further rich and beautiful affirmations, both of the Fathers of the Church and of the most ancient liturgical texts which emphasize the fact of the presence of the angels at Baptism, the sacrament of our "rebirth in Christ."[224]

Clearly, though, no less important than the presence of angels at our Baptism is the fact that the moment of our death,

---

[221] *Gelasian Sacramentary*, ed. Wilson, Oxford, 1984, p. 48.

[222] Origen, *Hom. in Jos.* IX, 4: PG 12, 874A.

[223] St. Ambrose, *De Sacr.* IV, 2, 5; Cf. also *De Myst.* 35, 36 (1 Peter 1:12).

[224] Particularly interesting in this regard are liturgical texts containing prayers calling for the purification of the baptismal waters through the angel of the Lord. Cf. Tertullian, *De Baptismo* 34, 35; Optatus of Milevis, *Contra Parmenianum* 11.6; *Gelasian Sacramentary*, cit. supra, p. 116; *Autun Sacramentary*, PL 72, 274D.

our second and true birth into eternal life, was seen by the Fathers of the Church as an event attended by the angels.

Tertullian, for example, wrote as follows: "When, through the power of death, the soul is separated from the mass of the body and springs up towards the pure, simple and serene light, the soul's angel exults and jumps with joy at the realization as it accompanies the soul to its eternal dwelling place."[225]

In his life of his sister, St. Macrina, St. Gregory of Nyssa put onto his dying sister's lips the following words: "Send to me the angel of light to guide me towards my place of solace, where are to be found the waters of rest."[226]

And in the very ancient *Apostolic Constitutions*, we find the following prayer for the dying: "Turn your eyes to your servant. Pardon him if he has sinned and make the angels favor him."[227]

Thus, from the time of our birth on this earth until, following death, we make our own entrance into eternity, the angels are always with us. They help us throughout the course of our time here below "to live Christ" with that dynamism of faith, hope, and charity, of which the sacraments are the prime propellants.

4. *Presence of the Angels at the Eucharistic Sacrifice*

We are nourished by Christ, the Bread of Life, when we participate in the great sacrament par excellence: the Eucharist, summit and center of Christian worship. With this great sacrifice the angels are also associated.

In point of fact: "The Mass is a sacramental participation in the celestial liturgy, in the worship officially rendered to the Trinity through the spiritual creation."[228]

---

225 Quoted in Daniélou, op. cit., p. 119.

226 St. Gregory of Nyssa, PG 46, 984D.

227 *Apostolic Constitutions* VIII, 41.

228 Jean Daniélou, op. cit., p. 79.

Today we are so immersed in the socio-cultural reality of our day — indeed we are submerged almost entirely in those realities which can be perceived by the senses — that we all too easily risk participating in the eucharistic sacrifice with a degree of inattention actually inferior to that which we accord by a natural process of empathy, for example, to sports events or television programs.

It is therefore worthwhile to draw upon the "memory" of the Church expressed in the living Tradition of the Fathers in order to remind ourselves how the angels, always present at the eucharistic celebration, exulting in the praise and adoration that is underway, are capable of stimulating in us a spiritual attitude similar to their own.

St. John Chrysostom writes that "angels surround the celebrant. The sanctuary and the space around the altar are filled with celestial powers who are there to honor the One present on the altar."[229]

The presence of the angels at the eucharistic celebration is made explicit at peak moments in the liturgical rite.

The Oriental rites, always more expansive and prolonged in order to permit the worshippers to enter more fully into the presence of God, deliberately make more frequent mention of the angels than is the case in the Roman rite.

"With perfect art, the liturgy begins gradually by eliciting the attention, refining the faculties of the spirit, and causing them to tremble before the threshold of the mystery."[230]

In the "Simple Entrance," before the book of the Gospels is solemnly carried in procession, the liturgy quotes John: "Amen, amen, I say to you, you will see the heavens open, and the angels of God ascending and descending upon the Son of man."[231] To

[229] St. John Chrysostom, *De Sac.*, VI, 4.

[230] P. Evdokimov, *La Preghiera della Chiesa orientale* ["The Prayer of the Eastern Church"], Queriniana, Brescia, 1969, p. 44.

[231] John 1:51.

this, another New Testament verse provides this solemn response: "And from the throne came a voice crying: 'Praise our God, all you his servants...'"[232]

It is at this point that the earthly liturgy is joined to the celestial one, for the rite specifies: "Grant that with our own entrance the holy angels may enter in who celebrate and glorify your goodness along with us."

In the Liturgy of the Catechumens, there comes the great hymn or chant called the *Trisagion*, a typical expression of the praise of the thrice holy God; this is meant to arouse an experience in us of the wholly Other and to open in the depths of our hearts a place receptive to the mystery.

"You who are praised by the Seraphim as thrice holy, who are glorified by the Cherubim, and adored by all the celestial powers...."

It is believed that the angels, invoked directly as they are here, will purify the heart of everyone who sings the hymn through to the final doxology: "Holy God, Mighty God, God Immortal, be adored!"

This *Trisagion* is like "an atrium providing access to the Trinitarian mystery."[233] It plays this typical role not only in the eucharistic liturgy but in the entire Orthodox Sacred Office (the Liturgy of the Hours and various other prayers). It is also part of the funeral rite and is sometimes even chanted at times of natural disasters.

But how can we avoid speaking of yet another solemn moment in the Oriental eucharistic liturgy, namely, the *Cherubikon*? "We, who mystically represent the Cherubim and sing the hymn thrice holy to the lifegiving Trinity, set aside all worldly preoccupations in order to welcome the King of the universe, *invisibly escorted by the angelic hosts.*" Here, at this high

---

[232] Revelation 19:5.

[233] P. Evdokimov, op. cit., p. 158.

point of the liturgical action, the praise of the faithful is in a certain sense mystically identified with the praise of those "angels with many eyes and pulsating wings who are like a purifying breeze from on high."[234]

Again, the eucharistic *Anaphora*, the prayer of oblation recited by the priest, emphasizes the fact of an angelic presence: "We thank you for all your benefits, known and unknown to us... and also for this liturgy which we ask you to deign to receive from our hands, even though you are surrounded by myriads of angels who sing, acclaim, and cry out the triumphal hymn."

At this point the chorus comes in, almost as if to emphasize in a particularly solemn and powerful way the praise of the angels, which becomes also the praise of men: "Holy, holy, holy is the Lord of hosts!"[235]

If it is true that the relentless sweep of the minute hand pauses at noon in an act of adoring love, then it is equally true that where men are helped by the angels to enter more profoundly into the mystery of the liturgy par excellence, the liturgy redeems time itself and brings humankind into a state of harmony.

The reason for this is that the heavenly liturgy helps us to acquire a sense of how to act lovingly while awaiting eternal life.

From this point of view, how can we not recall that even in the Roman rite every Preface introduces the same high point of praise with expressions that are more or less varied, each one nevertheless expressing the same fundamental concept: "United with all the choirs of angels in heaven, we proclaim your glory and join in their unending hymn of praise"?

In this regard we must ask ourselves: if the angels were to be eliminated as superstitious representations or burdensome fantasies from that treasure-house which is the faith of the

---

[234] Ibid., p. 181.

[235] Cf. Ibid., p. 182 (Isaiah 6:3).

Church, what sense would it make to introduce them into this most solemn moment of the highest possible expression of the faith of the Church itself?

In conclusion to what has been set forth in this chapter, I would like to quote the theologian Eric Peterson: "The whole universe participates in the worship and praise of God. The angels represent the most spiritual part of this universe. For this reason the hymn of the angels can never be forgotten or eliminated from the official worship of the Church. It, in fact, gives to her praise the depth and transcendence which the character of Christian revelation requires."[236]

At a time when man is more than ever confronted with the sheer breadth and extension of the cosmos, it is not only significant that he should link his praise of God in the highest expression of worship to that of the angels, but it is perfectly in keeping with the cosmic dimensions of his knowledge and existential experience.

Nor does certain criticism of the new Roman Missal — criticism which maintains that, in comparison with that of Pius V, the new Missal has downplayed the role of the angels at Mass and sidelined them in the faith of the People of God — make any sense.

The liturgist P.M. Quay, in a very careful article examining the new Missal and its Prefaces issued in 1970 and 1975, concluded, rather, that far from negating or neglecting the existence of the angels, the new Roman Missal speaks of the angels in such a way as to bring out better than ever before their true role in the economy of salvation; this emphasis, moreover, has been entirely in keeping with those modern theological investigations which have attempted to throw greater light on God's overall plan for mankind.[237]

---

[236] E. Peterson, op. cit., p. 57.

[237] P.M. Quay, "Angels and Demons in the New 'Missale Romanum,'" in *Ephemerides Liturgicae*, 459 (1980), pp. 401-409.

5. *Angels in the Text of the Roman Liturgy*

The Mass represents the action of God's grace par excellence; it is the summit of the Christian liturgy.

The angels, as we have seen, represent the bridge between the celestial liturgy (as we are told in the Book of Revelation) and the high point of the earthly liturgy. The one gets caught up in the other so to speak. The individual who truly prays with the Church is aware of being immersed in a mystery filled with the glory of God, not least of all because the angels themselves are celebrating and singing the praises of God along with him.

As the author of the Letter to the Hebrews expresses it, the whole of the Christian life becomes liturgical action. He, in fact, makes us aware that, unlike the Old Covenant, the New Covenant intimately introduces us into the family of God: "But you have come to Mount Zion and to the city of the living God, the heavenly Jerusalem, and to innumerable angels in festal gathering, and to the assembly of the firstborn who are enrolled in heaven, and to God who is judge of all...."[238]

It is precisely because life and liturgy are so inextricably related to one another — indeed they shape one another in the true spirit of Christ — that the Church uses the liturgy to educate us, as the old adage states: *Lex orandi, lex credendi* ["The rule of prayer is the rule of belief" or, to put it in other words, "As one prays, so one believes"]. Particularly significant for our argument, of course, are the feast days especially dedicated to the angels: September 29, the feast of the three Archangels, of whom we have already spoken at length in this book, St. Michael, St. Gabriel, and St. Raphael; and October 2, the feast of the Guardian Angels. To these special feasts must be added the Mass in honor of all the angels.

When you come to think of it, the liturgy always represents a pedagogical occasion for the Church.

---

[238] Hebrews 12:22-23.

The Church reminds us in the liturgy that the angels do in fact exist and that for the faithful to venerate them means, very concretely, to be put in a position to be helped by them in realizing the plan of God which, for us, of course, consists of salvation in Jesus Christ the Redeemer.

It is no accident that, in the Mass of the three Archangels, as well as the one in honor of all the holy angels, the Entrance Antiphon puts Psalm 102 on our lips: "Bless the Lord, all you his angels, mighty in power, you obey his Word, and heed the sound of his voice."[239]

The Opening Prayer, which is identical in the two Masses, has a clarity and coherence which does not admit of any doubts regarding its basic thrust. The Church firmly believes in the existence of these pure spirits who, far from being consigned to the sidelines of marginal popular devotions, are called upon to help us, as only they can, in a very powerful way to become what God wants us to become: "God our Father, in a wonderful way you guide the work of angels and men. May those who serve you constantly in heaven keep our lives safe from all harm on earth."[240]

The Opening Prayer of the feast of the Guardian Angels expresses itself this way: "God our Father, in your loving Providence *you send your holy angels to watch over us*. Hear our prayers; defend us always by their protection and let us share your life with them forever." The Entrance Antiphon for this Mass uses an expression from the Canticle of Daniel, again associating the praise of God rendered on earth with that given him in heaven: "Bless the Lord, all you angels of the Lord. Sing his glory and praise forever."[241]

The Responsorial Psalm for the feast of the three Archan-

[239] Entrance Antiphon for Sts. Michael, Gabriel, and Raphael based on Psalm 102:20.

[240] Opening Prayer for the Mass of the Archangels and of the Holy Angels.

[241] Opening Prayer and Entrance Antiphon for the feast of the Guardian Angels.

gels repeats the theme of singing the praises of God "in the sight of the angels." For the feast of the Guardian Angels, however, the Responsorial Psalm puts emphasis on the cry of joy and praise for the Lord who gives help and protection by putting "his angels in charge of you, to guard you in all your ways."[242]

The Gospel Alleluia is identical in both of these Masses and is based on Psalm 103: "Bless the Lord, all you his angels, his ministers who do his will."[243]

Emphasizing the fact that the angels adhere totally to the will of God, and that their praise is for that reason true, this liturgical expression stimulates us to become ourselves a "living praise of God" by virtue of our fulfillment of his will, day by day.

That the Church's offering might be taken up and carried to God "by the ministry of [his] angels... [to] be pleasing to [him] and helpful to our salvation"[244] where it becomes for all the source of pardon and deliverance is a prayer which opens our hearts and helps us to accept the ministry of the angels precisely in the sense that for this we need to pray, purify ourselves, and unite ourselves to God.

The Prayer over the Gifts in the Mass of the Guardian Angels again makes reference to the tasks assigned to these angels in our regard, specifically those of guarding, defending, and directing us aright; this prayer also asks that the angels "keep us free from danger in this life and bring us to the joy of eternal life, where Jesus is Lord forever and ever."[245]

Similarly, the idea that the angels sustain us in our difficult pilgrimage towards our celestial homeland is emphasized in the prayer after Communion in each Mass. Formulated differently for each of the two Masses, they nevertheless bring out this teaching of the Church: the food which fortifies us for our

---

[242] Cf. Psalm 91:11.

[243] Psalm 103:21.

[244] Prayer over the Gifts, Mass of the Archangels.

[245] Prayer over the Gifts, Mass of the Guardian Angels

pilgrim way here below is the eucharistic bread, but the mysterious character of that particular bread does not exclude the fact that there is another gift from the goodness of the Father in our regard: it is "the watchful care of the angels" by which we can "advance along the way of salvation."

There is such joy contained in this truth of the faith that, opportunely, the Church makes the Communion Antiphon one in which the desire "to sing your praises *in the sight of the angels*" represents a veritable explosion of spiritual youth which the sacred mysteries have renewed.[246]

If each one of these liturgical texts is a compendium of truth expressed in prayer, then it is also true that the Preface, identical for the two Masses, introduces the splendor of certitude in the heart of the eucharistic celebration.

This Preface says: "Father, all-powerful and ever-living God, we do well always and everywhere to give you thanks. In praising your faithful angels and archangels, we also praise your glory, for in honoring them, we honor you, their Creator. Their splendor shows us your greatness, which surpasses in goodness the whole of creation. Through Christ our Lord the great army of angels rejoices in your glory. In adoration and joy we make their hymn of praise our own: Holy, holy, holy Lord...."

Without analyzing this Preface in depth, we are still amazed at the glimpse it affords us, even in our blindness, of God's eternal splendor.

In her liturgy, albeit with moderation, the Church sets the angels before us for our prayerful consideration.

Their very existence and presence tends to amplify in the heart of the believer the perception of the thrice-holy God, and to arouse a more lively appreciation and admiration of the infinity of his greatness as well as of his salvific love which is also manifested by means of this message.

A final liturgical mention of the angels is to be found in the

---

[246] Communion Antiphon for both feasts based on Psalm 137:1.

Night Prayer of the Liturgy of the Hours. On solemnities that do not occur on Sundays, the Church places this invocation on our lips: "We beg you to visit this house and banish from it all the deadly power of the enemy. *May your holy angels dwell here to keep us in peace,* and may your blessing be upon us always."

We cannot really believe in a God who is more a "boss," an impassive and unmoved judge, than a Father.

It is unfortunately true that there is embedded in the fabric of the world and of human life a mysterious "knot" which indicates the presence of Satan with his temptations and suggestions to do evil. And the darkness of the night, even psychologically, makes us fearful of getting tied up in this "knot." Nevertheless the liturgy arouses in us a strong hope: God, through the ministry of his angels, can deliver us from evil with the power of a love that reconciles and saves.

"We beg you to visit this house... May your holy angels dwell herein." These are two invocations which intermingle in the same very human feeling generated by the state of mind aroused in us by consideration of the dark side of our lives. These two invocations possess meaning and arouse an echoing response only in those who truly believe in God, in his Christ, and his Church; and who accept the truth of the existence of Satan, the great adversary, against whom the good angels contend in the same way that the rays of dawn contend against the lingering darkness of the night.

As the liturgy provides prayers for the ending of the day, it does the same for the ending of this life. These particular prayers also place before us the consoling presence of the angels.

The liturgy places on the lips of the priest who is praying for someone on the point of death the following tender expression: "Come to meet him (her), angels of the Lord! Receive his (her) soul and present him (her) to God the Most High."[247]

[247] Prayer for the Commendation of the Dying, "Prayer after Death."

Again for those on the verge of passing from this life, the Intercessions included with the Evening Prayer of the Divine Office prompt us to pray: "Accept, O Lord, the groans of the dying. May your holy angel visit and comfort them." The Liturgy of the Hours is typically quite frugal in its mention of the angels, but it always speaks of them without reticence or embarrassment as real spiritual beings.

Why then, it must be asked, is there such silence about the angels today in catechesis and education for the Christian life?

Perhaps what Pavel Evdokimov said regarding the Gospel texts applies equally to these precious biblical-liturgical texts on the angels: "We have submerged them in some kind of neutralizing solution. Everything which is striking, outside sensible experience and above the sense of the masses is sterilized. Our religion is thus flattened out, rendered prudent and in all things made reasonable. And, precisely for that reason, man rejects it."[248]

[248] P. Evdokimov, *L'amore folle di Dio* ["Inordinate Love of God"], Ed.Paoline, Rome, 1980, p. 160.

5

ANGELS IN OUR PERSONAL LIFE

1. A Guardian Angel for Everyone

Charles de Foucauld, an outstanding Christian speaking about the friendship and universal brotherhood which ought to distinguish every follower of Christ, even in his thoughts, once wrote: "In everyone you have some very powerful yet very loving friends because you have in them (or at least with them or against them) their own good Guardian Angels. Let your thoughts, then, be all sweetness, tenderness and peace."[249]

This is an important quotation, especially if we consider it along with the views of those who have consistently drawn their positions from the authentic springs of Christian tradition. At a time of decline in a society that basks in its goods and material reassurances (paying the penalty with unrest, violence, and desperation), to recover the limpid current of belief in the Guardian Angels seems to me especially important.

Let us, therefore, move from this testimony of a modern spiritual writer to a consideration of the views of others farther back in time.

Patristic tradition is rich in affirmations concerning the

---

[249] Charles de Foucauld, *Scritti Spirituali* ["Spiritual Writings"]. 9/11, *"Al ultimo posto. Ritiri in Terra Santa* ["In Last Place. Retreats in the Holy Land"], 1897-1900, Citta Nuova, Rome, 1974, p. 77.

Guardian Angels notwithstanding the fact that, from an exegetical point of view today, their interpretations of certain biblical passages in favor of the angels are somewhat forced.[250]

Other biblical texts, on the other hand, on which most of the Fathers of the Church relied heavily, are quite explicit about the mission which the angels received from God to assist in the salvation of each and every individual. It would be foolish to exclude them.[251] We need think only of what Jesus himself said about his "little ones": "I tell you that their angels in heaven always behold my Father's face."[252]

In the Acts of the Apostles, Rhoda, the servant girl who announced to the faithful Peter's exodus from prison was not only not believed; she was told by the others: "It is his angel!"[253]

On the basis of such biblical passages as these, but also probably of a strong oral tradition, Origen was able to write as follows: "Everyone of the faithful, we are told, however insignificant he may be in the Church, is assisted by an angel, and Christ is our witness that these angels behold the Father's face continually."[254]

But even before Origen, towards the end of the 1st century and at the beginning of the 2nd, in that most ancient collection of Christian writings known as the "Apostolic Fathers," pseudo-Barnabas and Hermas, whom we have already quoted, both spoke of the angels.[255]

Later, during the Patristic Golden Age, St. Basil the Great

---

[250] A.M. Canopi, op. cit., p. 14; M. Flick-Z. Alszeghy, op. cit., pp. 562-568; 681-683.

[251] This how St. Hilary of Poitiers described the ministry of the Guardian Angels: "It is not God who has need of their intercession, but rather our weakness. They are, in fact, sent for the benefit of those who are to inherit salvation, since nothing of what we do is hidden from God, and our infirmity is in need of a ministry" (*Tract. Super Ps. 128:7*).

[252] Matthew 18:10.

[253] Cf. Acts 12:13-15.

[254] Origen, *De Princ.* II, 10, 7.

[255] Cf. J. Daniélou, op. cit., p. 87.

affirmed that "an angel is assigned to every believer, unless we drive him away through sin. He guards the soul like an army on alert."[256] Basing himself on a text from the Psalms, St. Hilary wrote in the same vein: "All the faithful are helped in a very considerable way by these divine messengers in accordance with what has been written, namely, that the angel of the Lord stays near to those who fear the Lord."[257]

Summing up the opinion of many of the ancient Fathers of the Church,[258] St. Thomas Aquinas in his *Summa Theologica*[259] emphasized that an angel is assigned to every person at the time of his birth. But at the same time, out of envy for that individual's calling to the eternal felicity which he himself has lost, a demon likewise immediately begins to rage around the new born babe.

Then, after each Christian is baptized, the strength of Christ bursts into his life and, as a result, "the good angel becomes more powerful and more able to defend the soul confided to him by Christ."[260]

Origen, again, made an observation which fits the case exactly: "Christ who has redeemed the baptized person with his own blood and freed him from his wicked masters, entrusts him, now a believer in God, to a holy angel who, on account of his purity, continually looks upon the face of the Father."[261]

One authoritative voice on the modern theological scene has been without a doubt that of Karl Rahner who, on the subject of the Guardian Angels, wrote: "The liturgy and pious tradition both affirm the existence of the Guardian Angels; in other words, liturgy and tradition have made concrete the union

---

[256] St. Basil, *Hom. in Ps. 33:6.*

[257] St. Hilary of Poitiers, *Tract. super Ps. 124* (PL 9, 682BC).

[258] Cf. Clement of Alexandria, *Eclog.* 50; Tertullian, *De Anima,* XXXVII, 1; Origen, *In Jo. Comm.*, XIII, 49; St. Methodius of Olympus, *Conv.* II, 6.

[259] St. Thomas Aquinas, *Summa Theologica* I, q. 9, a. 113, ad 5.

[260] Cf. St. Basil, *Comm. in Is.* VIII, 207.

[261] Origen, *Comm. in Matt.* XIII, 28.

existing between men and angels in the one history of salvation, placing specific angels in relationship with specific human beings. Providing that we do not try to visualize this relationship in too anthropomorphic or infantile a manner, no objection is to be lodged against this kind of preaching."[262]

Of all the authors we have been citing here on the subject of the Guardian Angels, and the weight they normally carry in the exposition and elaboration of Christian doctrine generally, what Karl Rahner goes on to say carries special weight: "It is from Christology that this subject derives its ultimate significance and complexity."[263]

Our Guardian Angel is thus not some mythical surrogate of God, but a real spiritual being so entirely at God's service that the Lord has involved him in the great adventure of our salvation who are assigned to him out of God's own goodness and Providence.

One particular role of the Guardian Angel, of course, is to be God's messenger, bringing good inspirations, suggesting what God really wants from us.

Our Guardian Angel protects us from internal and external disturbances.

When St. John Chrysostom called the Guardian Angel an "angel of peace," he had this in mind.[264]

The Guardian Angel helps reprove and punish us when we have strayed from the right path. That is one of the reasons why Hermas called the Guardian Angel an "angel of repentance."[265]

The Guardian Angel facilitates and assists us in our first and most important task of all, that of praying. Hence, Tertullian called him the "angel of prayer."[266]

---

262 K. Rahner, op. cit., p. 116.

263 Ibid., p. 123.

264 Cf. *The Shepherd*, Vision V, 7.

265 St. John Chrysostom, *Serm. Asc.* 50.

266 Tertullian, *De Orat.* 16, 6.

We must dwell, even if only briefly, upon each one of these various aspects of the truth about our Guardian Angels.

Not for the sake of hair splitting or out of a taste for quibbling over theological fine-points, but rather out of a genuine need to breathe interiorly the true atmosphere of the salvation which Christ has gained for us do we do this. We do it, indeed, to strengthen and discipline our desire to live in Christ, with Christ, and through Christ in the sight of the Father.

2. *Angels of Peace*

In this day and age, the sun is setting on our civilization and we are only beginning to perceive some signs, like the tips of icebergs in a choppy sea, of the culture which will replace it. Precisely because we live in such a transitional period from a socio-cultural point of view, our times are more than ever marked by tension, apprehension, and violence.

Contemporary man is paying a price for this, living a life which is all too often filled with anxiety, stress and uncertainties of all kinds.

Never before, in fact, have neuroses and psychoses been the order of the day to the same extent they are today. Why, then, do we not have recourse more frequently to therapies of a spiritual nature rather than limiting ourselves to those which are purely medical — not only to cure, but to try to prevent these evils? The fact of the matter is that it is in the spirit that we notice the greatest disturbances today (just consider our society's massive incapacity to love as indicated by the failure of so many modern marriages). If the problems are spiritual, then, the attempted remedies should also be spiritual.

Recourse to the Lord Jesus, faith in the power of his Name and Spirit, are essential to our salvation. But precisely because this necessary recourse to Jesus can become too familiar, even casual, recourse to the Guardian Angels can be that much more useful.

It has been said that "life does not consist only of what is absolutely necessary; there is a broad area containing things that are neither necessary nor particularly useful. They simply serve. And they serve, in fact, to insure that the necessary does not become useless."[267]

With respect to urging people in a profitable way to abandon themselves completely to God's will — without fear, without delay, and without mental reservations, particularly, without deficiencies in faith — I believe devotion to the Guardian Angel is a particularly useful devotion today. This is all the more true if we consider the Guardian Angel under the aspect of that peace which is so congenial to him and to us, so necessary, and today so threatened.

"The good angel," wrote Hermas in *The Shepherd,* "is sensitive, modest, sweet, calm...; the wicked angel, by contrast, is prone to anger, is bitter and rash. When anger or bitterness takes possession of you, know that an evil angel is within you!"[268]

The idea that demons cast the human spirit into a sea of agitation and uncertainty is a sentiment also found in St. Athanasius, who adds: "Good angels always act peacefully and sweetly, inspiring joy and exultation."[269]

St. Gregory of Nyssa gave voice to exactly the same faith: "For those who are worthy of it, the Lord provides both life and peace through the instrumentality of his angels."[270]

And St. Basil exhorts us: "Let us pray to God, who is our friend, to send an angel of peace as our companion and in order to assist us."[271]

---

[267] S. Maggiolini, cited in F. Berra, *L'Angelo del Signore* ["The Angel of the Lord"], Ed. Sodalitas, Domodossola, 1974, p. 63.

[268] Hermas, *The Shepherd*, Precept VI, 2, 4.

[269] St. Athanasius, *Vita Antonii*, XXXV.

[270] St. Gregory of Nyssa, *Comm. in Cant.* 14.

[271] St. Basil, *Ep.* 1, 11.

We can understand, in view of all this testimony to an ancient and very clear belief in Guardian Angels, why St. Ignatius of Loyola, in times closer to our own, should have made use of the same concept in his "Rule for the Discernment of Spirits." This is what he wrote: "It is God and his angels in their movements who provide us with true joy and spiritual exultation, casting out all the sadness and disturbances stirred up by the enemy."[272]

It was not by chance that the author of the Letter to the Hebrews made clear that the angels are "ministering spirits sent forth to serve, for the sake of those who are to obtain salvation."[273]

Perhaps it is precisely our own age which has been called to rediscover the Guardian Angels as beings who are in the service of man's total salvation, including his proper equilibrium and peace here below.

Maybe now, more than ever, it is important that every time we feel ourselves tense or anxious or in any way disturbed, we should have immediate recourse to the angel of the Lord, to the angel into whose care God has entrusted us.

Especially in the morning, before the occupations and activities of the day begin, or in the evening when fatigue and similar pressures assail us, recourse to our Guardian Angel can be like drawing on the life-giving waters of personal peace.

3. *Angels of Repentance*

"There is joy before the angels of God over one sinner who repents."[274] The Fathers of the Church based their idea that the angels, and in particular the Guardian Angels, had the task of

[272] St. Ignatius of Loyola, *Spiritual Exercises*, 329.

[273] Hebrews 1:14.

[274] Luke 15:10.

inspiring in us both penitence and conversion on this biblical passage. In a permissive era such as our own, when the line of demarcation between good and evil has been blurred if not blotted out entirely, how encouraging it is to rediscover this aspect of the ministry of the angels in our regard!

Already in the apocalyptic Jewish work entitled the Book of Enoch, there was an angel named Fanuel who "presided over repentance for the hope of those who were to inherit eternal life."[275]

And likewise in that very ancient work of Christian faith already mentioned entitled *The Shepherd*, its author Hermas speaks at length of an "Angel of Repentance."

Especially interesting for us is the warning which Hermas gave to those who said they wanted to observe the commandments of God but who feared the dominion of the devil: "The devil is unable to dominate the servants of God if from the bottom of their heart they hope in God. The devil has the power to fight, but not to win. If, then, you offer him resistance, he will flee far from you. Those who are conceited, however, fear the devil as if he had been invested with real power. Take, for example, the case of a man who has filled an entire assortment of jars with good wine, among them some which are not entirely full. If he comes to check on his jars, he does not occupy himself with the ones which are already full; rather, he provides for the ones which are not yet full, fearing that if the wine in these becomes acidic, it will lose its savor.

"The same thing applies to the devil: he naturally tries to tempt all the servants of God. Those who are strong in the faith, however, resist him energetically and in such a way that, when the devil fails to get at them, he flees from them.

"At that point the devil proceeds to those who are not filled to the brim with faith, and here he finds an opening into which

[275] In J. Daniélou, op. cit., p. 95.

he throws himself, doing as he wills with them, even to the point of reducing them to becoming his slaves."[276]

The action of this Angel of Repentance who inspires penitence in us is described by Origen: "We are trained by the angels... In the first place, we are not castigated by the Father of the family but rather by the Guardian Angels who have been given the responsibility to castigate and correct each one of us. And it is better that we should be reprimanded by one of them."[277] As the modern theologian Cipriano Vagaggini[278] wrote in this regard: "The Angel of Repentance not only discloses our sins, but he plays a part in their remission."[279]

The idea that there exists an angel who moves us towards conversion and who corrects us because he wishes us well is an idea reiterated by Clement of Alexandria: "He who has been approached by the Angel of Repentance will no longer have to repent when he leaves his body; nor will he have to blush when the Lord himself comes to the feast accompanied by his angelic hosts."[280]

St. Hilary of Poitiers writes: "It is by means of the ministry of the angels that the raising of our affairs in heaven is procured."[281]

To this St. Gregory of Nyssa adds: "They represent the real levers sent to assist those destined for eternal salvation; as such they raise us up to the height of virtue."[282]

It is a matter of great consolation and light to know that, behind our remorse there is often an angel stirring up a certain

---

[276] Hermas, *The Shepherd*, Precept V.

[277] Origen, *Sel. in Ps. 37.*

[278] C. Vagaggini, *Il senso teologico della liturgia* ["The Theological Meaning of the Liturgy"], Ed. Paoline, Rome, 1965, p. 341.

[279] Vagaggini here cites a fundamental text in angelology, that of E. Peterson.

[280] Quoted by J. Daniélou, op. cit., p. 96.

[281] St. Hilary of Poitiers, *Tract. Super Ps. 120.*

[282] St. Gregory of Nyssa, *Vita di Mosè* ["Life of Moses"], PG 44, 384B.

interior "stagnation" in us, not to make us anxious, but to provoke in us a greater commitment to living an authentic Christian life.

4. *Angels of Prayer*

Another salient characteristic of our age is the rediscovery of prayer, though obviously not throughout the whole of our society. Nevertheless — in a way that is often quite lively and decisive in its expression, especially where it is proposed to young people "to pray the Word of God" — prayer, which not only forms the Christian but also contributes to "the harmonious growth of the individual, *homo faber and homo sapiens,* according to the person's fullest capacity and measure,"[283] has seen a resurgence of popularity in our time.

However, if there ever was an era when the contemplative style of prayer was aspired after but found difficult to achieve, it is surely our own. Though drowning in the messages of the mass media, we feel the fascination, as well as the fear of silence, and we have the unfortunate inclination in our culture to kill silence wherever it occurs, with CDs, loudspeakers, TVs and radios.

Without silence, however, it is simply impossible for any really profound prayer to take root — just as jonquils cannot grow in dry, rocky ground.

Here, then, are the things we want to focus on: whether the teacher of prayer is always the Lord Jesus; whether it is the Father who draws us to himself[284]; and whether it is the Holy Spirit who "intercedes in us with inexpressible groanings,"[285]

---

[283] C.M. Martini, *La dimensione contemplativa della vita* ["The Contemplative Dimension of Life"], Letter to the Clergy and Faithful of the Archdiocese of Milan for the Pastoral Year 1980-81, Milan, 1980, p. 13.

[284] "No one can come to me unless the Father who sent me draws him" (John 6:44).

[285] Romans 8:27.

without minimizing the enormous help the angels can be in our life of prayer.

Especially today, it would seem that a major task of the angels is to help us who call upon them to clear our psyches of such obstacles to prayer as fantasy, imagination and worldly preoccupations which keep us bogged down in sensible realities which, as we suggested above, typically involve us in constant movement and ceaseless chatter.

In the past certain practices in the spiritual life may have been guilty of an excessive "spiritualism" or even of a kind of "angelism"; they tended in many cases to confuse the differences between ourselves, who are incarnate spirits, with the angels, who are pure spirits. From this confusion came a certain negative emphasis which belittled the flesh and fostered a kind of flight from the world.

In contrast to such a totally otherworldly approach, the Second Vatican Council restored a healthy spirituality of the Incarnation. As followers of Christ, we remain faithful to God by being diligent in our worldly commitments, attentive to contemporary events, and concerned about the persons and things we encounter here below, while continuing to love with an overflowing love the One "who was and is and is to come."[286]

It is in the carrying out of this difficult balancing act that the mission of the angels in general and of the Guardian Angels in particular is inserted. We have already had occasion to note how, in the Book of Revelation, the angels present to God the prayers of the just. It is surely not out of place to observe that this entire final book of the New Testament takes place, so to speak, in the ambience of a liturgy of cosmic proportions embracing all eternity, in which the angels pray, praise, and adore God and the Lamb, all the while extending a helping hand to us here on earth to assist us in our own prayer, so that we too might enter along with them into communion with the God of our salvation. The

[286] Revelation 4:8.

thought of the Fathers of the Church is explicitly based on these biblical indications.

Clement of Alexandria, for example, speaks of "the angels who are at the service of offering prayers,"[287] and claimed that when anyone prays alone he is accompanied by a choir of angels.[288]

Tertullian, for his part, spoke of "the Angel of Prayer" who is present when prayers are offered up in the presence of the living God.[289]

Origen went so far as to say: "When a man prays to God, the angels gather about him and join him in his prayer. And not only that. Every Christian — even those who are quite insignificant in the Church — has an angel of his own, who looks on our Father's face in heaven and sees the Creator's divinity all the time. These angels pray with us and work with us, as far as they can, to obtain for us the things we ask for."[290]

It was Origen, again, who stressed that "the angel of the Lord wraps in the mantle of his protection, and defends whoever fears the Lord. The angel who continually contemplates the face of the Father in heaven continually presents his prayers to the God of the universe through the unique High Priest, uniting himself at the same time to the prayers of the one confided to his care."[291]

In particular, it was the common teaching of the Fathers of the Church that the angels participate in the official prayer of the Church which is the Liturgy of Hours.

Saint Benedict wrote as follows in his famous Rule: "We believe that God is present everywhere and that in every place

287 Clement of Alexandria, *Excerpt*. 27

288 Ibid., *Strom*. VII, 12.

289 Tertullian, *De Orat*. 16.

290 Origen, *De. Orat*. II, 5.

291 Origen, *Contra Celsus* VII, 36.

the eyes of God observe the good and the evil; more than ever, and with prior faith, we must believe this when we are engaged in the work of God. It is for this reason that we remind ourselves of what the prophet said: 'Serve the Lord with fear.' Or again: 'With wisdom sing God's praises. In the presence of the angels, I will sing my psalm to him.' We must reflect therefore how we must stand before God and the angels and sing in such a way that the mind is in accord with what the voice is saying."[292]

Paul the Deacon, the best of the ancient commentators on St. Benedict's Rule, wrote as follows concerning this particular passage: "This can be understood in two ways: first of all, if God is present, the angels are present too while we sing our psalms, for God is never without these messengers of his; the other way is that if the heart truly agrees with what the mouth is speaking, then our attitude is similar to that of the angels."[293]

The knowledge that our Guardian Angel joins us in our effort to pray is more consoling than ever, especially today.

All the angels, but especially our Guardian Angels, are our friends and powerful allies in bringing our prayer to God's ear.

Permit me to quote St. Augustine again on this matter: "[The angels] are so on fire with a holy love of God's beauty, so spiritual, unchangeable, and ineffable, that they hold in disdain all things — including themselves — which are less than divine, so that, with every grace that makes them good, they may rejoice in the Giver of all goodness, God.

"Actually, their knowledge, even of the world of time and change, is greater than the demons' because, in the Word of God, through whom the world was made, they contemplate the ultimate reasons why, in the cosmic order, some things can be used while others are refused, and nothing is confused... This special privilege of such knowledge God has rightly reserved to

---

[292] *Rule of St. Benedict*, 19.

[293] *Commentarius Pauli Warnefridi in S. Regulam*, Montecassino, 1880, p. 256.

the holy angels. Thus, they are not only eternal but also blessed. And the good which gives them blessedness is God Himself who created them, for their perfect and unfailing bliss is to share in the vision of God."[294]

To be aware, to the extent possible, of the powerful companionship of the angels (and especially that of our Guardian Angel) is to facilitate our passage into the contemplative dimension of life which right now is their beatitude and the reason for our hope.

This needs to be done without our ever losing sight of those temporal matters which, facilitated by the angels, we must approve, reprove, and always order in the interest of our own last end: the eternal and joyous contemplation of God who is Love.

[294] St. Augustine, *The City of God*, 9, 22.

6

ANGELS, OUR COMPANIONS IN ETERNITY

1. Angels and the Parousia

To look at this life without the prospect of eternity is like looking at the sea with a bad case of myopia. One risks mistaking it for a pond.

The perspective which the Bible provides us regarding the angels is not limited to their mission to us on our way to heaven, but also embraces the eschatological wonders at the end of time when "God will be all in all" and salvation history will find its ultimate fulfillment.

Only then will we finally be "at home." Only then will the angels have completed their mission in our regard. All that will remain to them then will be to go on singing and adoring without end the thrice holy God. Our job, when our transfiguration into the image of the risen Christ will have been fully realized, will be to join in their song of praise, to harmonize our voices with theirs, so to speak. "For in the resurrection [we] neither marry nor are given in marriage but are like angels in heaven."[295]

[295] Matthew 22:30.

The angels are the purest reflection of the beauty and holiness of God. We human beings, too, are a reflection — albeit a different reflection — of God, once, that is, we have definitively recovered the "image and likeness" of the One who created us out of love in innocence and integrity in the Garden of Eden and, again, out of love allowed his Son to come under the power of death in order that we might be brought back to life from the death of sin.

The Book of Revelation describes this triumphal marital reunion in which Christ the Bridegroom becomes one with his purified Bride, the holy Church of God.

"And from the throne came a voice saying, 'Praise our God, all you his servants, and all who fear him, small and great.' Then I heard what seemed to be the voice of a great multitude, like the sound of many waters and of mighty thunder peals, crying, 'Alleluia! For the Lord our God the Almighty reigns. Let us rejoice and exult and give him the glory, for the marriage of the Lamb has come, and his Bride has made herself ready; it was granted to her to be clothed with fine linen, bright and pure.'"[296]

This climax in the history of salvation was preceded by other moments which we may call "acts" of the same great drama.

"For the Lord himself will descend from heaven with a cry of command, with the Archangel's call, and with the sound of the trumpet of God. And the dead in Christ will rise first."[297]

Following this intervention of the angels with regard to the resurrection of the dead, they are also to be associated with the Last Judgment.

Jesus speaks of this under the veil of a parable: "The Kingdom of heaven is like a dragnet cast into the sea which gathered fish of every sort; when it was full, they drew it ashore,

[296] Revelation 19:5-8.

[297] 1 Thessalonians 4:16.

sat down and sorted the good into baskets but threw away the bad. So it will be at the end of the age. The angels will go out and sort the evil from the righteous."[298]

Jesus spoke even more explicitly about that decisive moment of "sorting out," when the angels will appear to execute the Last Judgment: "Then the sign of the Son of Man will appear in heaven, and all the tribes of the earth will mourn, and they will see the Son of Man coming on the clouds of heaven with great power and glory. And he will send out his angels with a loud trumpet call, and they will gather his elect from the four winds, from one end of heaven to the other."[299]

We will limit ourselves to citing in a footnote the multiple biblical references regarding this aspect of the Day of the Lord which associates the angels with the decisive moments of this eschatological event as ministers of the resurrection of the dead, of the great assembly of the elect, and of the separation of the just from the unjust.[300]

The most ancient tradition of the Church confirms the fact that the angels will be present as an integral part of this eschatological reality.

It will suffice to quote St. Ephraem the Syrian on this topic: "At that time the Lord will appear like lightning in the sky in indescribable glory. The angels and the archangels will go before him like burning and incandescent flames. The cherubim will incline their heads. The seraphim will fly everywhere, crying out: 'Raise yourselves up, you who are sleeping. The Bridegroom is coming!' Then tombs will open and in the twinkling of an eye, all the people will rise up and will see the holy beauty of the Bridegroom."[301]

---

[298] Matthew 13:47-49.

[299] Matthew 24:30-31.

[300] Cf. Matthew 13:40-41; 2 Thessalonians 1:7; Revelation 14, 15, 16, 20:12 ff.

[301] St. Ephraem, *Sec. Adv.* VII, 11.

St. Cyril of Jerusalem emphasized the majesty of this final court scene, when innumerable angels will be present along with all the human beings who ever lived, from the time of Adam on: "You will see, O man, before what a crowd of witnesses you will have to present yourself at the judgment. Every race of men will be present. Try to imagine in your mind all those who have lived from Adam until now. It will be an immense throng. Yet it will still be less than the number of angels present, who will be even more numerous... It was written that the number would be a thousand times a thousand not because this designated the actual number, but because the author could not express a greater number."[302]

When the resurrection and the judgment have taken place, after "the angels have hastened from every direction to lead all the saints and the faithful into glory,"[303] then will come the day without end, the full realization of the glory that awaits us.

St. Gregory of Nyssa tells us clearly: "When grace will have united men and angels, they will re-echo the hymn of praise."[304]

2. *Praise: The Eternal Communion of Angels and Men in God Who Is Love*

Our earthly destiny as "pilgrims of the Absolute" will only be reached in the fullness of joy in the praise of God when, having attained our final goal in heaven, there will follow an eternal day free of all darkness, pain and death.

At that point we will not have become angels ourselves, but we will be associated with them. We will finally be creatures in harmony with all because we will be fully "extended" in the

---

[302] St. Cyril of Jerusalem, *Cat. XV*, 24.

[303] St. Ephraem, *Sec. Adv.* III, 149.

[304] St. Gregory of Nyssa, *Hom. in Ps.* 9.

blessedness of praise. For the moment, we are still pilgrims on our way, though we know this to be our goal. The author of the Letter to Hebrews tells us clearly that here "we have no lasting city, but we seek the city which is to come."[305] Day after day, then, we make our approach to "Mount Zion and to the city of the living God, the heavenly Jerusalem, and to innumerable angels in festal gathering, and to the assembly of the firstborn who are enrolled in heaven."[306]

Today, many people have lost hope precisely because the sense of life as a pilgrimage towards a heavenly feast has been lost.

We are no longer pilgrims. The temptation to accumulate, to possess, to squeeze out of life every possible pleasure (as if the whole meaning of our existence consisted in putting down roots here below) all are proving to be terribly alienating.

Anyone who stresses the primacy of "having" over "being" is bound (little by little) to lose his identity, with all the aberrations and desperation that follows.

It is therefore urgent that we recover the sense of being on pilgrimage to the heavenly Jerusalem, called to take part in the joyful assembly of the angels and of the just gathered around God and the Lamb: the Christ "in whom we have redemption, the forgiveness of sins,"[307] who is our "bright morning star."[308]

Only from the prospect of eternity can the brief course of our earthly life be redeemed from absurdity, sadness, and perdition, and rise to the true meaning of a liturgy which inaugurates, in the tension of faith, hope, and love, what will eventually be realized fully in the beatific vision.

Those who are truly fulfilled are the saints, and this is

---

[305] Hebrews 13:14.

[306] Hebrews 12:22-24.

[307] Colossians 1:14.

[308] Revelation 22:16.

because their entire life is spent realizing God's plan for them. But what is this plan in the final analysis? We read what it is in that book regarding the Last Things, the Book of Revelation:

"All the angels... the elders, and the four living creatures, fell down and worshipped God who is seated on the throne, saying, 'Amen, Alleluia.' And from the throne came a voice crying, 'Praise our God, all you his servants....'"[309]

From the point of view of praise, what Pavel Evdokimov has written is very much to the point: "The saint is not a superman, but rather someone who lives out his truth as a liturgical being. The Fathers of the Church found the best anthropological definition in the phrase 'eucharistic adoration.' The human being is a man of the 'Sanctus' in his similarity to the choirs of angels who, in an eternally unchangeable gesture, stand around the living God engaged in singing and blessing with a threefold benediction the three faces of the one God."[310]

In effect, this is the fundamental vocation of man: to see himself as loved by God who is Love and, at the same time, to give love to his fellows, being aware of having been "sealed with the promised Holy Spirit... the pledge that we shall gain our inheritance when God redeems what He has acquired, to the praise of his glory."[311]

In order that we may one day become beings of praise forever in eternal glory, it is necessary that we be such now in the offering of our love.

All the law and the prophets are summed up in this one precept: "You shall love your neighbor as yourself" and "Love is the fulfillment of the law."[312]

At the end of our lives, as we can read in the Gospel according to Matthew (25:41, 45), our final examination will be

[309] Revelation 7:11; 19:45.

[310] P. Evdokimov, *Teologia della bellezza* ["Theology of Beauty"], p. 42.

[311] Ephesians 1:14, 13.

[312] Matthew 22:40; Romans 13:8.

on love: "As you did it to one of the least of these my brethren, you did it to me"; or again, "As you did not do it to one of the least of these, you did not do it to me." Through this sieve the great sifting out will take place which will decide the whole question of our eternal salvation.

As we have seen, the angels — diligent during our earthly life in urging us to open ourselves up to God and to commit ourselves to love in order to be true and authentic in the praise we render — will themselves take part in the drama of that decisive moment.

We must be attentive to what will occur when the angels, the supreme point of creation, involve in the fullness of praise, not only human beings, but the entire cosmos.

This will constitute the full glorification of God the Creator. "Worthy are you, Lord our God, to receive glory and honor and power, for you created all things, because of your will they came to be and were created,"[313] will be sung by the four living creatures, "full of eyes in front and behind" who preside over the governance of the physical world.[314]

The whole creation which, as the First Letter of Clement says, "is filled with the glory of God,"[315] will take part in the new heavens and the new earth, transfigured in the immense hymn of praise to the glory of God sung by the angels.

"The voice of many angels, numbering myriads of myriads and thousands of thousands..."[316] will sing out, "Worthy is the Lamb who was slain, to receive power and wealth and wisdom and might and honor and glory and blessing."[317] It will be the solemn yet joyful celebration of Christ and his Redemption, truly a "new song" with which we too will be associated. Gazing

---

[313] Revelation 4:11.

[314] Revelation 4:6 (See also the Jerusalem Bible note on this passage).

[315] Quoted by E. Peterson, op. cit., p. 42.

[316] Revelation 5:11.

[317] Revelation 5:12.

on the scroll which has been unsealed,[318] we shall marvel at the wonderful fabric of Providence and the significance of everything in life and in the universe which has been penetrated with the blood of Christ and hence been redeemed and granted salvation.

At that point we shall finally be satisfied; we too will have become love, and for always. For now, though, the Kingdom of God is like the first rays of dawn breaking over a land where rocks and thorns continue to do battle with the "seed" of the Word and where Satan still has power to stint its full growth and expansion.

All of us, together with the whole of creation, wait "with eager longing for the revelation of the sons of God; for creation was made subject to futility, not of its own will but by the will of him who subjected it, in hope that creation itself would be set free from its bondage to decay and share in the glorious liberty of the children of God."[319]

This expectation of ours is called Hope. We know that what has been revealed in the Word is true. And in point of fact, the things that have been announced for us really are "things into which the angels long to look."[320]

The interpretation given to these words of Peter by St. Hilary are quite interesting: "The object of this desire of the angels is nothing other than the beatitude of men... The angels want to see fulfilled what was promised by the preaching of the Gospel. For when these promises have fully come to pass the angels will be called to render thanks along with us by means of the gift of beatitude."[321] "Then," St. Gregory of Nyssa adds, "the joy of the angels will be great indeed when they see the unity of

[318] Cf. Revelation 5:9-10.

[319] Romans 8:19-21.

[320] 1 Peter 1:12.

[321] Quoted by J. Daniélou, op. cit., p. 138.

God's spiritual creation reconstituted... At that point, in an eminent way, they will present for us the action of grace to the One who, through Christ his firstborn, will have brought humanity back home again after it had been lost."[322]

Even in this life we learn that the foundation of being is love and the desire for communion because God, our Creator and Redeemer, is one in Three Persons who infinitely love one another.

When in "the new heavens and the new earth" all the temptations, contradictions, failures, falls, pains, anguish, and death connected with this life shall finally have been dissolved like vapors in the warm sun of eternity, and Satan shall have been definitively defeated, then we shall truly become that divinized humanity which "like a glass lantern will itself irradiate light."[323]

In our new mode of existing, in an ecstasy of love without end, the Bridegroom will be one with us and we will be one with the Bridegroom.

Our marriage will finally be consummated in its fullness forever.

At that point, in God, we shall also know the angels as creatures different from us by nature, but — like us — lovers of the divine Love, as is eminently fitting for liturgical beings, beings made for praise.

We shall irradiate to one another the splendor of the glory of God, and the power of our praise will provide the energy of a joy without end for us.

In our present life that is what we thirst for.

It is not by chance that the epilogue to the Book of Revelation, which itself concludes the whole record of divine revelation, contains the following passage: "The Spirit and the bride

[322] Quoted by J. Daniélou, op. cit., p. 139.

[323] P. Evdokimov, op. cit., p. 43.

say, 'Come.' Let him who hears say, 'Come.' And let him who is thirsty come."[324]

We must perforce thirst for our encounter with the Lord to come, for his Kingdom which will be revealed, and for the joy that will burst forth in all its fullness.

Let us thirst for the living God and love him.

Let us thirst for the living God and serve him in serving our fellows.

Let us thirst for the living God and experience the power of his praise on earth in order to attain to the fullness of love in the eternal life of praise to come.

Perhaps the most hidden yet most important ministry of the angels, our companions of pure love, is precisely this: to help us first to thirst, then to channel our thirst, and finally, to give it its proper name: a "thirst for God, for the living God."[325]

---

[324] Revelation 22:17.

[325] Psalm 42:2; also 63:1.

COLLECTION OF TEXTS

After this effort to focus on a reality which, for the reasons mentioned in the text (along with others), has been blurred to the point where many consider it a marginal reality if not actually a foolish one, we offer here a selection of texts on the subject by some eminent authors.

The angels have been considered real, existing spiritual beings with an undoubted role to play in the economy of salvation by personalities of the caliber of St. Augustine and St. John Damascene from the world of patristics; and from the field of modern theology by a man of the stature of Hans Urs von Balthasar, called by Henri de Lubac "the most cultivated man of our time."

Eminently realistic educators such as St. John Bosco of the last century, and men of culture such as Giorgio La Pira in the present century, not only believed in the existence of angels, but expressly involved them in their educational, social, cultural, and political work.

Our desire is that those who read these pages will find in them additional arguments to help in the rediscovery of the angels within the marvelous universe of Creation and Redemption: our own life and hope.

The point of rediscovering the angels is not to make them ornaments of our faith, or even dazzling stars at the center of its drama. No. The angels need to be rediscovered for what they really are, namely, pure spirits charged with a "ministry" by a God who is truly in love with man. The angels are "sent to serve man" with respect to the most fundamental problem facing him, namely, his own eternal salvation (cf. Hebrews 1:14).

ST. AUGUSTINE

Augustine represents one of the "summits" of human thought.

Born in Tagaste in Numidia in the year 354, he died as bishop of Hippo in the year 430; he had a profound influence on the whole of the development of Western civilization through his numerous works such as *The Confessions*, the story of his conversion; *The City of God; On the Trinity;* and numerous other works in apologetics, dogmatics, polemics, exegesis, ethics, and so on. He plunged into the debate over human ideas making an absolutely essential contribution to civilization, one extending far beyond the confines of the faith alone.

The Angels' Knowledge of God

The holy angels gain a knowledge of God not by the spoken word but by the presence in their souls of that immutable Truth which is the only-begotten Word of God. They know this Word and the Father and their Holy Spirit, understanding that this Trinity is indivisible and that each of the Persons is substantial, although there are not three Gods but only one. They comprehend all this in such a way that it is better known to them than we are known to ourselves.

They also know every creature not merely in itself but, still better, in the wisdom of God, in the very art by which it was created. And, therefore, they know themselves better in God than as they are in themselves, although, of course, they have this knowledge, too. For, these angels were created and are something different from the One who created them. Therefore, in the sense I have explained above (11, 7), the knowledge which they have in Him is as clear as daylight, whereas what they have in themselves is like the twilight.

For there is a great difference between knowing something in the very idea according to which it was made and knowing it as it is in itself. For example, it is one thing to understand the straightness of a line or the correctness of a figure when seen by the intellect and another when traced in the sand. So, too, to know justice in the light of immutable Truth is different from knowing justice in the soul of a just man.

It is the same with all other things—as the firmament of the heavens between the waters above and those below; the gathering of the waters below, the appearance of the dry land, and the production of plants and trees; the creation of sun, moon, and stars; of land animals, of fowl, fish, and of sea monsters; of all creatures that walk and crawl upon the earth; and of man himself who was to excel all that is upon the earth. All these are known by the angels in one way as the things are in the Word of God, where the angels see the unchangeable and eternal purposes and the ideas according to which all these things are in themselves. In the one case, the knowledge has the clarity of the Artist's thought; in the other, it has the shadows of the thing produced. But, when these creations are referred to the praise and adoration of the Creator Himself, it is as if the morning dawned in the minds of those who were contemplating them.

St. Augustine, *The City of God* in The Fathers of the Church, Vol. 14, New York, NY, 1952, Bk. XI, ch. 29, pp. 234-235.

ST. JOHN DAMASCENE

St. John Damascene, the last great theologian of the Greek Church, lived between 675 and 749. He spent a large part of his life in prayer, applying himself also to the tasks of preaching and writing. He entered the monastery of Mar Saba near Jerusalem, was ordained a priest there, and wrote his principal work there: *The Fount of Knowledge* of which his "Exposition of the Orthodox Faith" forms a part.

The Angels: Secondary Lights

The angel is immortal, not by nature, but by grace; for, naturally, everything that has beginning has an end, too. Only God is always existing—rather, transcends always, because He who made time is not subject to time but transcends it.

The angels are secondary spiritual lights, who receive their brightness from the first Light which is without beginning. They have no need of tongue and hearing; rather, they communicate their individual thoughts and designs to one another without having recourse to the spoken word.

Now, all the angels were created by the Word and perfected by the sanctification of the Holy Spirit, and in accordance with their dignity and rank they enjoy brightness and grace.

The angels are circumscribed, because when they are in heaven they are not on earth, and when they are sent to earth by God they do not remain in heaven. However, they are not confined by walls or doors or bars or seals, because they are unbounded. I say that they are unbounded, because they do not appear exactly as they are to the just and to them that God wills them to appear to. On the contrary, they appear under such a different form as can be seen by those who behold them. Of course, only the Uncreated is by nature unbounded, for all creation is bounded by God who created it.

The angels do not receive their sanctification by the Spirit as something due their essence. It is by the grace of God that they prophesy. They have no need of marriage, precisely because they are not mortal.

Since they are intellects, they are in places intellectually and are not corporeally circumscribed. For by nature they do not have bodily shape and they are not extended in three dimensions; rather, they are present and act in space intellectually in whatsoever place they are commanded to do so, and they are not able to be present and act in different places at the same time.

Whether the angels are equal in essence or whether they differ from one another we do not know. Only God knows, who made them and knows all things. They do, however, differ from one another in brightness and station, either having their station in accordance with their brightness or enjoying their brightness in accordance with their station. They illuminate one another by the excellence of their rank or nature. Moreover, it is evident that the more excellent communicate their brightness and their knowledge to them who are inferior.

They are vigorous and prompt in the execution of the divine will and by a natural quickness they appear immediately in whatever place the divine pleasure may command. They watch over the parts of the earth and are set over nations and places in accordance with their disposition by the Creator. They direct our affairs and help us. Moreover, they are ever round about God for the very reason that in accordance with the divine will and command they are above us.

From *St. John of Damascus, Writings,* The Fathers of the Church, Vol. 37, New York, NY, 1958, pp. 206-207.

PSEUDO-DIONYSIUS THE AREOPAGITE

Under the name of Dionysius, referring to a member of the Areopagus of Athens who was converted by St. Paul (cf. Acts 17), an unknown writer who wrote towards the end of the 5th or the beginning of the 6th century penned a series of works of great importance for the mystical theology of the Middle Ages. His work on the angels, *The Celestial Hierarchy*, is especially well-known; for many centuries it was the text most often consulted on the subject of the angels.

Images of God

The celestial spirits enjoy a higher participation in the gifts of the Trinity than do those beings which simply exist or are irrational or which reason as we do. Those things which mould them in an intelligible way after God through imitation and which cause them to resemble, in a supernatural way, the Thearchy (the Trinity of God as opposed to the hierarchy of the angels), by making every effort to conform their intelligence to that naturally more profound likeness, are their contacts with the Thearchy. The angels, in fact, live in communion with the Triune God and, to the extent that they consent, they tend on high, driven by divine and everlasting love, receiving primordial illumination in an immaterial way and without any admixture of darkness. Moreover they find this illumination connatural since their whole life is nothing other than intellection.

Such are the heavenly spirits, before all others and in many different ways participators in the divine and witnesses to the secrets of the Triune God. For this reason, in preference to all others, they were judged worthy of being called "angels." It is to them, before all others, that the illumination of the Thearchy comes and it is by means of them that those revelations which transcend us come down to us.

From Pseudo-Dionysius the Areopagite, *La Gerarchia Celeste*, 4, 2 in *La Teologia dei Padri*, I, Città Nuova, Rome, 1974, p. 144.

JOHANNES TAULER

Johannes Tauler, one of the greatest of the German mystics, was born in Strasbourg in 1300 and died there in 1361. He entered the Dominican Order when he was quite young and studied in Cologne, which was one of the greatest centers of theological education at that time. Disciple and defender of Meister Eckhart, he was also a friend of the Blessed Suso. With regard to the angels, his thought reflected the common opinion of the theologians and mystics of his time.

Angels: Watchful of God and Men

The Gospel tells us: "Their angels always look upon the face of my Father in heaven." I am not sure what words can and ought to be used to speak of these pure spirits, because they have neither hands or feet, figure, form or matter; and a being which has none of these things can hardly be grasped by thought or sense. How can one speak, then, of what they are? We don't know. Nor should that surprise us since we don't even know ourselves or our own spirit which makes us human beings and through which we possess anything of worth. How could we, then, know these noble and excellent spirits, whose nobility exceeds by much all the nobility which the whole world put together can offer? And so we speak about their activity in us and not about their essence. In fact, their activity consists in that they continually contemplate us and watch us in the mirror of divinity, formally, essentially, actually and distinctly. And they exercise a special and well defined work in us. Without doubt, God acts incessantly in us much more literally and nobly, but the angels cooperate in this work of God within us....

Each human being has a particular angel which has been given to him or her at Baptism, and to each angel a person has been assigned such that this angel is perpetually at his side, never to abandon him. And he watches over him, awake or asleep, in all his ways and works, both good and bad. And if one had no other reason to thank God and to love Him mightily than the fact that these high and noble creatures, superior to all knowledge being so elevated and unceasingly bound to us poor human beings, this one reason would be enough. In contrast, every human being likewise has a particular demon who is always pitted against him and who is as good at exercising influence over him as is his angel. If a person were wise and diligent, the opposition and temptations of the devil would be far more useful to him than the inspirations of the good angel. For if, in fact, there were no fight, there would be no victory.

Johannes Tauler, *Opere*, Edizioni Paoline,
Alba, 1977, pp. 527-528.

JOHN HENRY NEWMAN

Newman was a man of the greatest importance both in the Anglican and in the Catholic Churches. Born in London in 1801, he died in Birmingham in 1890, after having served Christ and the truth, often in situations where he was profoundly misunderstood. In making him a cardinal, Pope Leo XIII rendered homage to "the genius and doctrine" of one of the most significant personalities of the 19th century.

Executors of the Economy of God in Creation

I suppose it was to the Alexandrian school and to the early Church that I owe in particular what I definitely held about the angels. I viewed them, not only as the ministers employed by the Creator in the Jewish and Christian dispensations, as we find on the face of Scripture, but as carrying on, as Scripture also implies, the Economy of the Visible World. I considered them as the real causes of motion, light, and life, and of those elementary principles of the physical universe, which, when offered in their developments to our senses, suggest to us the notion of cause and effect, and of what are called the laws of nature.

I have drawn out this doctrine in my Sermon for Michaelmas day, written not later than 1834. I say of the angels, "Every breath of air and ray of light and heat, every beautiful prospect is, as it were, the skirts of their garments, the waving of the robes of those whose faces see God."

Again, I ask what would be the thoughts of a man who, "when examining a flower, or a herb, or a pebble, or a ray of light, which he treats as something so beneath him in the scale of existence, suddenly discovered that he was in the presence of some powerful being who was hidden behind the visible things he was inspecting, who, though concealing his wise hand, was giving them their beauty, grace, and perfection, as being God's instrument for the purpose, nay, whose robe and ornaments those objects were, which he was so eager to analyze?" and I therefore remark that "we may say with grateful and simple hearts with the Three Holy Children, 'O all ye works of the Lord... bless ye the Lord, praise Him, and magnify Him for ever.'"

From *Apologia pro Vita Sua,* Doubleday & Co., Inc., Garden City, NY, 1956, pp. 146-147.

ST. JOHN BOSCO

St. John Bosco (1815-1888) was better known as "the apostle of the 19th century," or even as "the apostle of youth," on account of his special charism in the Church of God, namely, that of collaborating with Christ in the salvation of the young, especially the poorest and most abandoned of them. Chiefly for them, he tried to encourage a sound press; he himself wrote works of apologetics and of popularization in the field of Christian doctrine.

The Dignity of Each Man Entrusted to the Guardian Angel

One argument that shows the excellence of man is surely the fact that he has an angel as a guardian.*

God who created the heavens and the earth and all of the things that are in the heavens and the earth allowed them to follow the natural laws established by his ordinary daily Providence which kept everything in being. This was not the way it was with man, however.

Besides having enriched him with noble faculties, both corporal and spiritual, and constituted him master over all the other creatures, God also wished that man should be taken care of by a celestial spirit. Thus, from the first moment of man's appearance on earth, an angel attends to him both night and day. This angel accompanies him in his walks along the street; defends and protects both his body and his spirit; prompts in him the knowledge of what is good so that he may follow it. All this points both to the great dignity of man and the great goodness of God. We have a most solemn duty to live up to all this!

* The idea of the Guardian Angel was so familiar to Don Bosco that, one day, hearing some workmen sing a song containing a very rhythmical refrain, he memorized the tune and wrote

down the notes of it. Then he asked Silvio Pellico to write some verses to the tune in invocation of the Guardian Angel. The poet accepted the proposal and wrote a song that actually became very popular and appealed greatly to the young.

From the Introduction to "The Devotee of the Guardian Angel" in *Memorie biografiche di san Giovanni Bosco* ["Biographical Memoirs of St. John Bosco"], collected by G.B. Lemoyne, II, Scuola Tipografica Salesiana, San Benigno, Canavese, 1901, p. 269.

PAUL CLAUDEL

Paul Claudel was born in 1866 and died in 1955. He was one of the most important French poets and essayists of the 20th century. After many unpredictable changes in both his life and his thought, he became a convert to Catholicism, eventually leaving many profoundly religious pages evidencing a very solid faith.

The Angels

Let us set aside once and for all the ignominy of materialism and cease seeing in our sensitive faculties which nature has provided us the cause of our knowledge whereas they are merely means and instruments.

Who cannot see how the body, by imposing on us its own conditions, is a hindrance to us? Between ourselves and all other beings there are always two mountains to scale, theirs and then our own. We only arrive at intimate reality in a doubtful manner, in an initial way, by conjecture and inference. Our senses come to a halt at the surface of things and leave to the spirit the job of continuing on as it can. But a ray of sunlight does not pass through a pane of glass more quickly, nor does water fill a glass more exactly than a being who is nothing but spirit can impregnate, or better, possess, or espouse not only the form but fully and intelligently that complex of forces and energies by which the form is maintained vis-a-vis its subject.

The most beloved being is nothing more than a looking glass which attracts, arrests and repulses us at the same time. But there is nothing that an angel, if we open our hearts to him, cannot touch in us or is incapable of associating to his freedom which is the privilege of the children of God.

He is the contemporary of our origin and the contemporary of our reason for being. He knows us, not by partial contact or through the elaboration of conventional signs which our minds interpret, but through a total application of his being to ours, as a musical note is modified completely in its substance by means of a change in the key signature.

Man exists to know; an angel knows to exist.

Man was made to render to God his consent, the free and intelligent homage of his will to the diverse plans of material creation which are juxtaposed and aligned under and around him till he meets with nothingness. An angel encounters God directly in his very reason for being and reproduces him, so to speak, like an open book solely because he is, realizing his being according to that particular mode by which he differs from all other beings.

The angel has nothing to learn: he knows and exists by watching... There is no veil. There is nothing in the angel which opposes the fulfillment of his person, of that for which he was made; neither ignorance, nor weakness, nor any other obstacle. Knowing is everything and is transformed immediately into willing like a closed circle.

He breathes inexhaustibly from the Breath of Life.

His vision exerts such a pull on his will, the Spirit draws his spirit with such force that the blending of all his infinitely complex and rhythmic elements issue directly from nothingness in the pronunciation of that wonderful Name, of Being without end.

Paul Claudel, *Note sugli Angeli* in *Presenza e Profezia*, Milan, 1959, pp. 169-172.

PAVEL EVDOKIMOV

He was born at St. Petersburg in 1901 (his father was assassinated when he was six years old). He died in France in 1970, after a career which established him as one of the most stimulating thinkers of our time. He began his theological studies in Kiev. Driven into exile, he worked as a taxi driver in Istanbul and later as a cook in Paris, where he also studied at the seminary of St. Sergius, where he later won renown as a teacher. He collaborated with the *Encyclopédie Française* as well as with numerous magazines and reviews, and also wrote some notable books, including *The Theology of Beauty* and *Gogol and Dostoevsky*. Olivier Clément considered him "one of the masters of theology and spirituality of the twentieth century."

The Angels at Work in the World

According to the Fathers of the Church, the angels personify heavenly powers and are stationed by God close to the people as their guides. In the same way, the Guardian Angel, unique and personal for each human being, carries God's thought to that person, the projected image of his sanctity, and is thus very intimately related to the person who is assigned to him. The angels take a fairly active part in the historic existence of the world, leading a battle under the direction of St. Michael the Archangel against the demons, those powers over nothing and apes of the angels, thus safeguarding the order of the cosmos.

After death, the "spirit-bearing" angels receive the soul as it leaves the body. According to St.Basil, the Angels of Judgment "weigh" the souls. These, who assist in every divine work, are especially present at the death of a martyr. Origen insists a great deal on their liturgical function; the angels surround the Trinity and concelebrate with Christ the divine liturgy.

Jacob's ladder shows them to be messengers of God. These are "glued" to the word and will of God and personify it. When

God decides to heal, his will takes the figure of the Angel Raphael. Every time an angel appears it is to transmit and fulfill God's will....

The angels reveal "heaven," in the way they exist and act coming as they do from God to men. While maintaining his power of direct revelation, most often God reveals himself by means of the angels who are the bearers of his energy, his light and his revelation. For example, when the three angels appeared to Abram in the plains of Mamre they are considered, above all in the iconographic tradition, as figures of the three divine persons, an icon of the Trinity. The angel is a locus of God's appearance to man, a living manifestation of God, the name of God is in him and with the name, God's presence.

Traditionally, the monastic life is compared to that of an angel. A holy monk is called an "earthly angel and a heavenly man." The spiritual life of man is related to the prayer and contemplative activity of the angels, "secondary lights...."

According to St. Basil, the Holy Spirit is the Spirit of communion and the angels are in a special way his servants when they lead men towards the communion of saints in the love of Christ.

P. Evdokimov, *La santitá nella tradizione della Chiesa ortodossa*, Ed. Esperienze, Fossano, 1977, pp. 126-127.

GIORGIO LA PIRA

Born in Pozzallo in Sicily in 1904, Giorgio La Pira died in Florence in August of 1977. He was one of the most prestigious Catholic figures of the present century. Prominent in both politics and culture, he operated in an environment that was not merely ecclesial but ecumenical as well, and this on a world scale. His collaborator and biographer, Fioretta Mazzei, wrote about him as follows: "He talked about angels even in the Kremlin; he spoke of the angels who watched over children and of the biblical angels of the cities who measured them from top to bottom, protected them from destruction, and collected their prayers in order to present them to the Lord" (F. Mazzei, *La Pira*, Ed. Fiorentina, Florence, 1981, p. 129).

2/10/51: Guardian Angels

My adoring Angel — the city of God where the angels adore, glorify, and infinitely love the Father, the Son, and the Holy Spirit. My Guardian Angel too forms part of this band of lovers and contemplatives. This eternal light and this eternal hymn reverberates over us if we are children: *Angeli enim eorum semper vident*, etc.

May I always remain under the reflection of this virginal light!

From: Unpublished "Personal Notes,"
kindly supplied by Fioretta Mazzei

Angels of the City

The revelation of both the Old and the New Testaments — and in general all the great religious traditions of humanity — assures us of an angelic protection that really does exist; it extends over individual persons and even over individual cities.

Our failure to pay attention to these fundamental values

which invisibly but very really lend such weight and purpose to the affairs of men has caused us to lose a true perception of the mystery of the city. Nevertheless the mystery does exist, and manifests itself today with signs which appear more and more unmistakable, calling for responsibility from each and every one.

From: *Il valore delle città* ["The Value of Cities"],
a speech of La Pira in Geneva,April 12, 1954,
unpublished; supplied by Fioretta Mazzei.

HANS URS VON BALTHASAR

This eminent Swiss theologian (1905-1988) was, according to Henri de Lubac, "the most cultivated man of his day." He brought together the most diverse currents of thought: from patristics to Greek and Latin authors to St. Thomas to modern French writers such as Claudel and Bernanos. From his major work, *The Glory of the Lord,* which presents the faith as the discovery of the immense glory of God, one and Triune, we present this excerpt on the angels.

Angels and the Son of Man

The angels — who played an increasingly gnoseological role in the Old Testament as intermediaries and who, according to late Judaism and St. Paul, were mediators of the covenant on Mount Sinai — in the New Covenant took on a merely secondary role in function of their service of accompaniment to the Son of Man on earth. Their mediation is no longer substantially necessary since the Son has the Father always at his side (cf. Jn 8:16; 16:32), where he rests in the bosom of the Father (cf. Jn 1:18) and even acts in virtue of power received from the Father (cf. Jn 5:22), beginning with his own seeing, listening and touching of the Father (cf. Jn 3:11; 8:26, 38). Nevertheless the angels can never be absent; in the first place, because they constitute such an integral part of the celestial glory of the Son of Man; and in the second place, and above all, because they are the ones who must make the social character of the Kingdom of heaven real — the Kingdom into which the entire cosmos must be transformed. It is not, nor should it appear to be, that the Kingdom which the Son came to found and which he certainly enfleshed in its totality (as an *autobasileia*) is an absolutely solitary place which would become populated by the community of those who would come after him. More truly, this place, in God, to which the redeemed of earth are to be conducted, was from the very beginning "the city of the living God, the heavenly Jerusalem," with its "countless hosts of angels, the festive community of the firstborn" (Heb 12:22-23).

As Powers on earth and in the heavenly cosmos, the angels have no need to endure and be subjected to the lot of suffering first (cf. Col 1:20).

The Son who, as God, is above them, accomplishes the work of the Redemption in that he is "ascendent," elevated above them (cf. Heb 1:4, 14). Precisely because of this, they are placed as his followers and are at his service: "Are not all angels spirits in the divine service, sent to serve for the sake of those who are to inherit salvation?" (Heb 1:14).

This, in so far as it witnesses to the living Kingdom of heaven, pertains to a form of glory for the Son of Man: "You will see the heavens open, and the angels of God ascending and descending on the Son of Man" (Jn 1:51). This expression, which without doubt harkens back to the vision of Jacob (in which the ascent is recorded before the descent), is never substantially fulfilled in John.

It is necessary, then, to admit that John took up this image handed down (perhaps in the context of the relative eschatological image) as the theophany of God himself, as the glory of the Father in the Son. Even in the synoptics the angels are always absent when Jesus acts and speaks in the fullness of his power.

He does not have recourse to them, even in their role of servant. He could have had them from the Father in his prison, but he would not (cf. Mt 26:53). Nor would he walk with them in an air of dignity, as if they might complete his celestial figure as the two thieves completed his configuration on the cross. The angels follow his path but only as the splendor of the light which gives testimony to him.

According to Luke they appear at his crib as the splendor of his descent; after the Ascension they appear as the splendor of his ascent. In the empty tomb, they represent the splendor of his resurrection, which from within the empty tomb throws light on the past. After the temptation and the victory over the powers of the devil, they come forward to serve him (cf. Mt 4:11). Still in Luke, an angel appears to comfort him in the Garden of Olives where the Suffering Servant is completely submerged in human suffering; this almost Old Testament service of mediation in suffering is entirely plausible. Only in the eschatological image of the Son of Man who returns from heaven "with his angels," is the promised vision of John directly fulfilled. It is eschatological because is takes place at the same time as the apocalypse. Finally, the Book of Revelation allows us to catch a glimpse of the community of angels and men in the Jerusalem on high.

Hans Urs von Balthasar, *The Glory of the Lord,*
A Theological Aesthetics, Vol. 1: Seeing the Form,
T. and T. Clark, Edinburgh, 1982, pp. 632-634.

JEAN GUITTON

Born at St. Etienne on August 18, 1901, Jean Guitton was a student of Henri Bergson and one of the most representative Catholic thinkers of our day. He must be placed among the most important scholars to expound the relationship between every facet of Catholic and contemporary culture; he accomplished this with great acuity, always remaining relevant. Occupying himself with the most important theological questions, Guitton was a personality in whom the Catholic laity successfully expressed the faith in an entirely adult fashion; he himself incarnated the man of today and spoke efficaciously to modern man in a fashion that was always credible.

Angels

Do the angels truly exist? I always have in mind what Etienne Souriau, one of the most liberal of souls, professor of esthetics at the Sorbonne, answered: "Put the problem of their existence between parentheses. I limit myself to their significance. I retain that we are surrounded by angels, conveyers of beauty. There is an angel for every nation, every province, every man: the Guardian Angel."

He counseled me to recall those persons I may have met by chance, on a train or in the air, who spoke a meaningful word to me and then disappeared. Persons whom I never saw again but who, with a simple word, profoundly changed my life.

An angel is above all that visitor who announces an improbable stroke of good fortune. Many are the poets who have sung their praises: Vigny, Lamartine, Mallarmé himself, and Valéry whom Degas called an angel because he was, like Novalis, often caught out of himself and hyperlucid.

Let me go beyond these symbols. I believe in the angels, in their real existence. Sometimes I have thought to have sensed — above and most of all at my side — a being barely perceptible and secret, who removes obstacles, inspires me, protects me, and guides me. Who at times, with his finger to his lips, brings me a message with which I have to agree. I find that the scene of the Annunciation, in which Gabriel communicates with the Virgin only to ask her to say, "Yes," is repeated often in human lives.

In Jesus' agony, when he was abandoned, the angel fulfills in his regard the role of consoler. And I suppose that Christ crucified was invisibly surrounded, aided and consoled by these announcers of joy.

I have been asked myself how an artist — a painter or a sculptor — should represent these invisible beings. It is not easy. Beato Angelico, who painted the angels of music, made only pallid impressions. Gustave Moreau is perhaps in our time, the best portrayer of the angels. The angel is androgynous, composed of sweetness and vigor. His wings are like external lungs. His hair, rays of the sun. His face is pure light. He has no members. He is a flame.

One might think that a sculptor would do better here than the painter. On the door of the cathedral, an angel can make even the stones smile. The smile is a sign of the spirit on his face. The angel knows. The angel is silent. He only reveals himself by means of his smile.

From the *Osservatore Romano*, March 21-22, 1983.

TO THE ANGELS

From inside our closed dwelling
where too often we play
at a pretence of life,
prisoners of goods
transitory and deceiving,
seize us,
angels,
shining companions
of immaterial strength and beauty.
In your being
as whirlpools of light
around "the One who is,
who was, and who is to come,"
we too can be attracted
and polarized
and centered in him
with both mind and heart
down to the roots of our being.
From our impenetrable dwellings
where the "I" is sick with gloom
and always more enfeebled,
closed in and worn out with goods,
asphalt and straw,
you must free us then, angels,
our vigilant and loving companions.
In your being as spirals of light
around the One who is "the First and the Last,
the Alpha and Omega, the Beginning and the End"
of each most hidden desire of the human heart
and of history and of the universe,
we too can be attracted
and vivified
and pacified
to the point that we too become
lives of praise of his immense glory.

TO THE GUARDIAN ANGEL

In your silence
my distracted life comes together again
like calm coming over the waves
at the time of dying light.
In your prayer
my infinite thirst is appeased
like a sudden spring of water gushing out
on the slope of a dry mountain.
In your love
my heart brightens up with trust
like a lamp lighted up
by the fluid of the oil dripping down into it.
O Angel of praise
and of eternal contemplation,
adoring Angel,
take in the hollow of your pure hand
the flicker of my brief life
and make of it a "hosanna" of fire
that will never be extinguished.